Mungo MacCallum is a journalist and
author whose most recent books are
Mungo: the man who laughs and *Girt by Sea*.

HOW TO BE A MEGALOMANIAC

HOW TO BE A MEGALOMANIAC

or

Advice To A Young Politician

MUNGO MacCALLUM

DUFFY & SNELLGROVE
SYDNEY

Published by Duffy & Snellgrove in 2002
PO Box 177 Potts Point NSW 1335 Australia
info@duffyandsnellgrove.com.au

Distributed by Pan Macmillan

© Mungo MacCallum 2002

Cartoons by Patrick Cook
Cover design by Alex Snellgrove
Typeset by Cooper Graphics
Printed by Griffin Press

ISBN 1 876631 54 6

visit our website: www.duffyandsnellgrove.com.au

CONTENTS

*For all the good politicians — the ones who ignore
this advice and remember that power
is not an end in itself but a means to a better world.*

If the road to hell is paved with good intentions,
are bad intentions the pathway to paradise?

And if people leave politics to spend
more time with their families, do they go
into politics to spend less?

INTRODUCTION

In spite of the title, this book is not some kind of Machiavellian primer; it is satire, albeit satire with a warning. One of the reasons politics in Australia is currently at such a low ebb, and politicians so despised by the public at large, is that so many of the current crop seem intent on taking the advice of cynics like Uncle Mungo. Perhaps this book will help both voters and decent politicians to recognise the symptoms and to weed them out before they do any more damage.

The form is unashamedly pinched from *The Screwtape Letters* by C.S. Lewis, a religious allegory in which an old devil instructs a young devil in how to tempt human souls to their damnation. In my version the old devil is, of course, Uncle Mungo; he is not I. I still regard politics as a necessary and honourable trade and most politicians as well intentioned – at least at the start. Uncle Mungo is the Mr Hyde to my Dr Jekyll.

It is worth noting that the creator of the wonderful and terrible story of these characters, Robert Louis Stevenson, was himself an acute observer of politics. Among his other writings is this insight: 'Politics is perhaps the only profession for which no preparation is thought necessary.' If this book does little to correct this state of affairs, at least it may identify some of its pitfalls.

Mungo MacCallum

ONE

In which Terry Dobbin decides on a political career and Uncle Mungo makes some preliminary suggestions

My Dear Terry,

I must admit it was with some surprise that I read of your desire to make a career in politics. But after the laughter subsided and I realised that it was just possible that you were serious, I thought: the boy needs help. And I, having spent most of my working life as a fascinated, if sometimes disgusted, observer of the tragi-comic circus which comprises what Ambrose Bierce defined as 'a strife of interests masquerading as a contest of principles. The conduct of public affairs for private advantage' am of course in a uniquely privileged position to provide it. So, if you will just leave your wallet with the receptionist and lie down on this comfortable couch, let's get on with it.

First, let's be very clear about why you are attracted to the great game, or to the Australian version of it, which bears rather less resemblance to chess than it does to nude mud wrestling. I sincerely hope and trust that idealism plays no part in your ambitions, for if it does you are almost certain to be disappointed. There is, of course, a time and a place for idealism; no policy speech should be without it. But many long years have passed since it was a core element in the political process.

3

Many have noted that Thomas Jefferson, who penned the immortal line: 'We hold these truths to be self-evident; that all men are created equal ... ' was an unashamed slave owner. On a more mundane level one of Australia's own founding fathers asked the people to vote for the lofty aim of federation with the words: 'We shall found a great nation, and there will be cheaper meat.' Even Ben Chifley, arguably one of our most visionary prime ministers and certainly our best loved, observed trenchantly that the most sensitive part of the voter's anatomy was the hip pocket nerve.

The more successful of our politicians have seldom forgotten this revelation for very long. When Bob Hawke, then Australia's most popular political figure, was preparing for the election that brought him to power, he and his acolytes were keen to run on the themes of consensus and reconciliation until the street-hardened New South Wales premier, Neville Wran, brought them back to earth. 'Delegates,' he rasped, 'it's all very well to go on with all this spiritual stuff, but if those greedy bastards out there wanted spiritualism they'd join the fucking hari krishnas.' The campaign quickly reverted to the traditional promise of tax cuts.

So: when setting out your career path, just how much room should you allow for idealism? The hard answer is, not very much. Like love in an arranged marriage, there will be time for all that stuff later; the important thing is to get the basics right.

And before we go any further, I fear something must be done about your name. I am sure you have grown used to it, even attached to it; after all, it has been part of you since birth. But let me be brutally frank: Terence Urquhart Rupert

4

Dobbin does not really have a statesmanlike ring to it. Apart from the unfortunate acronym (and why give your colleagues a free kick with nicknames? They'll find plenty of scope for cruelty without it) there is a trivial, even plodding quality about it. Simply losing the middle names would not really help. You need something sharper, more straightforward and no nonsense.

Almost all Australian prime ministers have had first names which either started as one syllable or could be shortened to one: Bob, John, Ben, Joe, Jim, Bill – Billy was somehow acceptable. Those who didn't – Edmund Barton, Alfred Deakin, Stanley Bruce and Malcolm Fraser, for instance – generally either belonged to another age or looked as if they should have. If I might make a suggestion, Jack has come back into popularity and has an honest Aussie ring about it.

For a surname, two syllables are generally to be preferred, although Hawke and Howard (in strine at least) have managed with only one (but see below). The name should be recognisable, but not too common, with maybe just a hint of aristocracy about it to suggest that the bearer is serious: Fraser and Barton struck a nice balance. And of course it should not be too ethnic, a stricture which includes Irish and Scots as well as those more usually designated as New Australians. Bentley, for instance, would be splendid.

And don't overlook the value of a middle name, or even two, to give a touch of distinction. While John Howard sounds almost drab enough to fit its owner, John Winston Howard adds a totally undeserved *gravitas*. Similarly, plain old Bob Hawke is transformed into a man of the world as Robert James Lee Hawke. Kim Beazley was too frequently confused

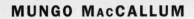

with his father and in any case never had sufficient oomph; but as Kim Christian Beazley he at least declared his allegiance to a declining, but still powerful, constituency. The best example of all was Tom Hughes, who sounded like something out of *Tom Brown's Schooldays* until, during his brief time in politics before deciding that being Australia's most expensive barrister was more fun, he was revealed as Thomas Eyre Forrest Hughes – definitely prime ministerial material. Look, therefore, for something of historical resonance – may I suggest a pinch from my own family? Jack Wentworth Bentley. It only remains to add the magic letters MP and you are in business.

You may have noticed that in all the above examples I have avoided one illustrious name, that of Edward Gough Whitlam. But then both the man and the name broke all the rules. And, it must be admitted, he remains an idealist to the end. All one can say is that he was a blinding exception, and one that may well be held up as an unreachable goal, but one that should not be emulated by any but the very brave or the very foolhardy. He was a giant in his day, but these are not the times to be larger than life.

Well, we've got the name out of the way; the next step is to find a party in which to insert it. I am glad to note that you have not mentioned any personal preference. This shows that you are realistic about keeping all your options open, a trait which has become essential for a successful career in mainstream politics.

You will not be surprised to learn that the major parties now employ talent scouts to search out bright young men and women, especially around the universities, with the aim of recruiting them before the other side does. These head-hunters are usually rather sad figures, those who have never quite made it themselves and see their footnote in history as being the one who discovered the Australian Napoleon; they also dream about having sex with the students, which, like their other ambition, seldom comes to pass. Still, they have been useful in persuading the politicians of tomorrow that they should forget principle at an early age and simply go to the party that offers the best deal.

It is not clear what eventually attracted Peter Costello to the Libs, and given the man's record in libel actions I am certainly not about to speculate, but it is a matter of record that he was at least playing footsy with the Labor Club during his days on campus; his co-litigant Tony Abbott was probably too busy playing punchy to indulge in such machinations. Thus the best way forward is to make some sort of name for yourself in some public cause – it doesn't really matter much which, as long as it gets you recognised – and let it be known that you are ready to consider approaches.

The alternative is to go to the trouble of joining a party on your own initiative, then turning up to branch meetings and making yourself useful until your fellow rank-and-filers offer you an honorary position in the branch as your first handhold on the greasy totem pole. This, however, is an incredibly boring ritual and you have to associate with a lot of losers on the way through. Far better to be chosen as an up-and-comer from the start.

It is also more sensible to aim for a major party from the beginning. Certainly the competition is tougher and the rules, both written and unwritten, more onerous, but remember that only two parties – Liberal and Labor – can ever hope to deliver to you the post of head of government. The others can provide a comfortable living, plenty of perks, lots of opportunities for travel and sex and, from time to time, a measure of real political power; but they can't put you in the top job. If that is your ultimate aim (and if it isn't you should probably consider a career in some less demanding field, like swimming naked with white pointers or the SAS) you will have to stick with the big two – or at least put yourself in a position to join one of them at some point in your career. This latter course is, however, not recommended. If you are tempted, think Cheryl Kernot and revert to plan A.

But wait, you may say. Look at some of the heavy hitters in recent years; look at the DLP, the Democrats, even an independent like Brian Harradine. They just about ran the country; on the big decisions they were more important than any senior minister. And what's more they never had to worry about all those tiresome bits like balancing the budget or what happens to the Aussie dollar. They just crashed the party whenever they felt like it and left the other buggers to clear up the mess: no care and still less responsibility. Isn't that the fun place to be?

Well, up to a point, although, as the abovementioned Cheryl found out, it's never enough for a genuine megalomaniac. But even being a maddening minority isn't that easy. Notice that all the above – the DLP, the Democrats and Harradine – are splinters from the major parties (or rats, to use the technical term). Even One Nation only appeared because Pauline Hanson was expelled from the Liberal Party for appearing too right wing in 1996 – within five years she had

become mainstream as she indignantly pointed out. Notice also that almost all their influence is negative: by voting with the opposition they can sometimes block government legislation, but they can never pass legislation of their own except by arrangement with the government, and this does not happen very often. Being a spoiler can appeal to a certain class of bastard, but I like to think that you have your mind set on far greater bastardries than that.

And remember: in a major party, if you get sick of it, you can always switch. Admittedly you are unlikely to get an opportunity like Billy Hughes, who strode majestically from being a Labor prime minister straight to being a Nationalist prime minister and ended his career with the boast that he had at least drawn the line at joining the Country Party. Nor is it probable that you could be plucked from a brawl in your own party to become the instant leader of the opposition, as happened to Joe Lyons. But never allow yourself to believe that your membership of a party represents an indissoluble tie, any more than you should align yourself with a particular candidate for the leadership. Malcolm Fraser had a happy form of words for the latter problem: he always maintained that the leader of the Liberal Party had his total and undivided loyalty, but he was always careful never to name the actual leader – until, of course, it was himself.

But this is all still ahead of you; the first thing to do is get a foot in the door. So back to the choice of a party. Many years ago I wrote that there was a more or less natural mix within the various parties: if you were a union official or a school teacher you would join the Labor Party, if you were a businessman or an independent shopkeeper the Liberals, if a farmer or rural worker the Nationals, and if you weren't quite sure what you were you would join the Democrats. If you were a lawyer, you could of course join anyone.

To some extent this process of natural selection still applies, but the rigidities have broken down considerably. These days the only party which can be said to have a really hidebound ideology is the Greens, where compromise is considered a form of treason, not merely to the party but to the planet; it is good to see that there is still a refuge left for fanatics. The others all like to describe themselves as 'broad churches', in which free and frank debate is encouraged and a range of dissenting voices tolerated, and there is plenty of room for flying pigs, too. In practice the ruling cliques lay down the guidelines, and the only real latitude you will receive is in the choice of which tie you wear with your soberly dark suit (the correct answer is yellow). Dissidents cannot actually be expelled from parliament (much as the bosses would like the power to do so) but they can be frozen into a corner in which any kind of promotion is impossible until the leadership changes.

These days this seldom happens without a change of government as well; but take heart. Although the last one seems an aeon away, changes of government at the federal level are actually fairly frequent, taking place on average about once every six years. It is true that the coalition had one stretch of 23 years and Labor one of 13; but these are balanced by some very short-lived regimes at the start of the century, and of course Gough Whitlam's spectacular, but brief, three years.

It is smart to try to make your own rise through the party coincide with the political cycle; if, for instance, you expect to be ready for the front bench in, say, 12 years, this may well be just when Labor is returning to government the time after next and if you have chosen to embrace the heirs of Curtin and Chifley, you may (hallelujah!) be in line for a ministry. If, on the other hand, you have picked the party of Menzies and Fraser, it may be another two terms before you can get your hands on the keys to the Lodge. This timetable is, of course, far from guaranteed, but it is one more factor to consider before taking the plunge.

Another, of course, is the competition, and I don't mean from the political opposition. The story is told of a newcomer taking his place for the first time in the House of Representatives. Settling gingerly into his seat he looked across the chamber. 'There they are,' he breathed. 'The enemy.' An old hand sitting near him smiled sardonically. 'No, son,' he replied. 'That's the opposition. The enemy are the ones sitting all round you.'

So, know your enemy. If you see the party of your choice recruiting lots of eager, energetic, well-qualified young talent, do not fall into the trap of thinking that this must be where the future lies, that this new generation will dominate the politics of the future and that you'd love to be part of the team. Think of them not as political allies, but as rivals for the ministry. Do you really want to have to fight your way through that lot?

Far better, perhaps, to look at the other side: a party down in the dumps, struggling to find anyone worthwhile to fill the gaps in its depleted ranks. It may well be in opposition for quite a while, but hey, you've got quite a while. And one thing is certain: it may take longer than average, but sooner or later it will be back in government, and by then you, largely through lack of competition, will be one of the senior people, a leading light whose passage to the ministry – and who knows, perhaps even to the very top – will be assured.

As long as you haven't done anything seriously offensive – such as challenging the current leadership before you have the numbers – your ascent is guaranteed. And the good thing is that you can get yourself into a position of dominance before the next wave of bright young things decides it's time to try to get on board. By then your seniority should ensure that you get promoted ahead of them anyway; but if it doesn't – if any of them look as if they could become a serious threat – you will be in a splendid position to sabotage their preselections and cut them off at the knees. There is a lot to be said for being top of your class, even if it is the worst class in living memory.

Of course, all this is only a rough guide – a sort of general primer for absolute beginners. Even at this early stage there is plenty of room to improvise, to seize chances as they occur and exploit whatever circumstances you may find yourself in. If you are the lad I think you are, you will quickly learn the value of opportunism. But do not become overenthusiastic too soon. It is true that one of the enduring slogans of Australian politics is: 'If you see a head, kick it.' Yes, but perhaps not quite yet; there will be plenty of time for that once you have become established. For one starting from the bottom a better motto might be: 'If you see an arse, kiss it.' While you are on the way up, you can never have too many allies. Cultivate them as much as you can for the moment; you can always shaft them later on. Their shocked expressions and howls of outrage will then be all the more satisfying. Why, I remember once Bob Hawke … but no, that's a story for another time. For the moment, just get yourself a name and a reputation, then hold your nose and dive right in.

And the very best of luck, Terry, or rather Jack – we might as well get used to it.

Regards from your voyeuristic uncle,
Mungo.

TWO

*In which Uncle Mungo discusses names, ideals,
and the creation of an acceptable past*

My Dear Jack – for I insist on addressing you as such, despite your understandable reluctance to abandon the name in which you were christened.

I know that you have made your reputation, such as it is, as Terry Dobbin – but of what does that really consist? A slightly better than average HSC pass, a couple of minor sports trophies, a stint in the boy scouts and, at least as far as we know, no criminal record. You are quite right in insisting that there is nothing here of which to feel ashamed; but let's face it, there is nothing to excite the imagination of the masses either.

I am not suggesting that it may become necessary to invent a whole new life history – such a course is fraught with danger, even in minor matters. You may recall a New South Wales Minister for Education, one William Davis-Hughes, who fraudulently awarded himself a Bachelor of Science degree; his hide was thick enough to resist exposure, but it hardly counted as a plus on his political *curriculum vitae*. Such risks should only be taken when there is more to be gained than personal ego boosting.

But a change of name involves little risk, and may even gain points for initiative. Davis-Hughes's own premier was

17

baptised Robin Askin, but he found the Christian name far too effete for the colourful racing identities that were his preferred company. Thus, in defiance of church law he became Robert, usually shortened to the bluff Bob. A similar course was adopted by the Labor Party's nemesis of the '50s and '60s. Bartholomew Augustine Michael Santamaria – although Bob Santamaria somehow never had the working-class ring of the average Carlton supporter the sinister Jesuit sought to portray.

You maintain that Terry Dobbin has a comfortable, unthreatening ring to it, and of course you are right. But this is part of the problem; it lacks a touch of steel, even of the lash. Voters indeed like to feel comfortable and relaxed, as John Howard promised before he began the most disruptive and divisive reign in modern Australian history – although of course there are also times when they yearn for that touch of excitement Paul Keating promised, and indeed delivered. But above all they need to know that they are in sure hands; that their leader is willing and able to make the hard decisions on their behalf, albeit never in a way that seriously impinges on their chosen lifestyle. Terry Dobbin promises repose and contentment; but Jack Wentworth Bentley adds the assurance of security and vigilance, with just a frisson (which is all that is needed or desirable) of vision. Please reconsider.

And while we are on the subject of meaningless abstractions and political clichés, I note with some apprehension that you have not abandoned idealism altogether; you simply assumed that I would take it for granted that your desire to enter politics was in fact a desire to contribute to a better world. This kind of generality is acceptable; after all, few politicians have risen to power by promising to contribute to a worse world – although Churchill's often misquoted offer to his constituents of 'blood and toil, tears and sweat' came perilously close. However, those were other times, the Poms have always had a far greater taste for masochism than the Australians, and in any case you are no Winston Churchill – and should not seek to be, either.

Especially not with a name like Dobbin, but I trust I have already made that point.

The desire to contribute to a better world no doubt does you credit, but it will only continue to do so as long as you keep your aims so vague as to be totally incapable of fulfilment. That way you can never be said to have comprehensively failed them. The worst risk a politician can take is to set himself a measurable target. It is also one of the few ways of actually achieving a result, but of course that is never the primary aim of any government which hopes to maintain power indefinitely, as all of them do.

Remember, and learn from, Bob Hawke's 'After 1990, no Australian child will live in poverty', or his equally grandiose pledge to plant one billion trees (the latter was not quite as disastrous, for the simple reason that the number is incomprehensible to the normal mind, and anyway, who's going to count them). Shudder as you recall Bob Carr's repeated vows to halve waiting lists for public hospitals.

On a slightly different level, cringe at the memory of every opposition leader's policy speech in recent years, with their invariable promises to end jobs for the boys and raise parliamentary standards. And of course, never ever say never ever. As John Howard will be the first to remind you, that was then, and this is now.

The broadest aims are the ones that wear best. In 1949 Robert Menzies promised to put the value back in the pound. If this meant anything (and there are plenty of economists who can prove it didn't) it presumably implied that the government would seek to revalue the currency against its trading partners, something which could be achieved with the stroke of a pen in those palmy days of fixed exchange rates, while simultaneously holding domestic inflation to something close to zero. The abovementioned economists will assure you that in the medium to long term the two aims are incompatible.

Menzies, who knew about as much about economics as he did about quasars (which hadn't even been discovered at the time) never had the faintest idea of how to go about fulfilling either of these aims. However he had inherited a red-hot team of financial whiz-kids from his Labor predecessors and was smart enough to ignore their obvious ideological differences in favour of their expertise. A pattern developed: Menzies would call in such luminaries as Roland Wilson, Richard Randall and H.C. 'Nugget' Coombs and lay out his general budgetary plans for the next fiscal period. He would then look expectantly at the troops, one of whom would reply: 'Prime Minister, you have told us what you wish to do. We will now tell you what you are able to do.' And they would, and he would do it.

Such lofty ambitions are still a long way beyond you, even if such a team of fearless and talented public servants was available to advise you — which, since the ruthless politicisation of the bureaucracy, which started with John Gorton and reached its numbing apotheosis under John Howard, is unlikely to be the case. But you get the general idea. Keep it vague to the point of inanity. But add, if you can, a personal touch. 'I only wish to contribute to a better world' is good, but 'I only wish to contribute to a better world for my children' is better. Perhaps best of all is 'I only wish to contribute to a better world for all our children'.

Going further tends to blur the message – no bad thing in itself, but it needs to be done for the right reasons. 'I only wish to contribute to a better world for all our children, and for all our children's children' certainly implies farsightedness (not to mention longevity) but may appear a fraction too ambitious. Remember that for most voters, the phrase 'the foreseeable future' means about the middle of next week or the arrival of the next pay packet, whichever comes sooner. A budgetary year is like a geological age, which is often a blessing in that politicians are seldom held responsible for anything much for longer than a few weeks, despite the frantic efforts of their opponents and of some determined sticklers in the media. This talent of the voting public for rapid forgiveness and forgetfulness is one for which we should all be profoundly grateful and one which should be assiduously exploited, but it should not, repeat not, be taken for granted.

Which brings us to the next stage of the transformation of Terry Dobbin, nonentity, into Jack Wentworth Bentley, politician extraordinaire. It is seldom a good idea to invent an entirely fictitious past; there is always the risk that it will be found out, as happened to that poor bastard of a television announcer in Darwin who claimed to have been a member of the Australian Olympic swimming team in Mexico. A direct lie is almost always a mistake, even in politics. But it can also be considered an unnecessary risk, as much can be implied and insinuated without recourse to absolute mendacity.

Let's face it, even Peter Reith seldom came out with a blatant fabrication, even after the giveaway phrase: 'Let me be perfectly frank …' emerged from his well-tended lips. However, while they were moving, the unvarnished truth was not all that came out. It was probably unfair of me to claim in one well-reasoned critique that Reith had a physical allergy to telling the truth, which brought him out in hives, although my evidence – that no one had ever seen Peter Reith with hives – was undoubtedly persuasive.

Have you perchance read a newspaper at some time in your brief career? If so that entitles you to claim that you were 'fascinated by politics from an early age'. Did you once buy a poppy on Remembrance Day, or a Legacy badge? If so, you are 'a tireless worker for charities, especially those concerned to repay the debt we owe to those gallant men and women who have fought and died to preserve our freedom'. As I recall the last time you went into a theatre was to have your tonsils removed, but you have been known to watch the late-night movie on television because you were too lazy to get up after the football finished. Thus, your 'devotion to the arts is matched only by your keen interest in all forms of sporting activity'. You see how simple it is.

Any association with the great and famous, however tenuous, must of course be advertised – even a rebuff can be turned to advantage with suitable phrasing. A slightly built Labor candidate named Ritchie Gun once claimed in an election pamphlet that Gough Whitlam had singled him out for praise for his wide range of knowledge. When others pointed out that the gigantic Whitlam, who frequently had

problems with short people, had done no such thing, Ritchie drew himself up to his full height (about a metre and a half) and replied indignantly: 'He certainly did. He once called me a little fucking know-all.'

Ritchie could also claim to be something of a wine connoisseur. Once, during a tasting at Parliament House, a fellow member asked him innocently: 'Where's Shiraz?' Ritchie responded immediately: 'I'm sitting on it.' But we digress. The point, as I'm sure you have gathered by now, is that it is easy to build a massively impressive past out of little more than an ability to stay awake for a brief period every day.

The other side of this is that it is almost inevitable there are things you would prefer to conceal, or at least gloss over. In politics, almost any departure from the conventional is suspect; eccentricity is generally to be avoided. The admission by Lady Alexandra Hasluck in *Who's Who* that her favourite occupation was 'searching country graveyards' may not have been as ghoulish as it sounded, but it certainly did her husband Sir Paul no good in his ultimately unsuccessful quest for the Liberal leadership.

There is, of course, a fine line. Senator Bill O'Chee made much of his success as a champion of some sort of sport involving tobogganing, surely an aberration on the least snowy continent on earth. But then, O'Chee was himself already an aberration in conservative politics by reason of his mixed Irish-Chinese ancestry (the Chinese part was all right, but the Libs have never had much time for the Irish).

Ancestry can be useful; as I have written elsewhere, an Aborigine or a convict somewhere in the family tree can these days be a social advantage rather than a drawback. It is still true that what is quaintly called an 'ethnic', as opposed to Anglo-Celtic, background is generally more acceptable to the Labor side of politics than to the Coalition, but the barriers can be broken down in special cases. Only last year Sophie Panopolous was rewarded for her outspoken monarchism with a Liberal seat in Victoria, and the Libs will remind you that the first Aborigine to sit in the federal parliament was one of them; at least he was until Neville Bonner began pushing the case for indigenous Australians and was promptly dumped to an unwinnable position on the Queensland senate ticket.

However, as far as we know you have nothing particularly unusual in the family bloodstream, and it is too much trouble to try to invent an interesting ancestor at this stage of your life. We shall have to be content with portraying you as an ordinary man – insofar, that is, as the outstandingly promising Jack Wentworth Bentley can ever be described as merely ordinary. Your ambition should be bright but not blinding, your aims lofty (and always vague) in scope, but modest in keeping with your still humble status on the totem pole.

It does no harm to hint that you are hoping for bigger things – every electorate likes to imagine that one day it will be represented by the prime minister. In this context a self-deprecating reference to the old line that every corporal carries a field marshal's baton in his rucksack often comes in handy – it was used frequently by the megalomaniacal Peter Reith, whom we have met before and will meet again as a useful exemplar of ruthless political self-interest. But always make it clear that your real purpose is no more or less than service – first to your electorate, then to your party and finally to the nation. Go no further; according to the current Australian doctrine, the rest of the world can bloody well look after itself.

These are the positives, which can be mastered by any tyro with lots of tickets on himself and a hide like a rhinoceros. But traps for the unwary remain. Back to those little peccadillos in the past which may, just possibly, be brought out by an opponent as unscrupulous as we hope to make you in a contest for pre-selection or, still worse, in the run-up to a real election for parliament.

Is there anything you would like to tell us? Are you sure? Not so much as a juvenile car theft, a suspended sentencing for break and enter, a small investment in a string of brothels? All of these and much worse can be glossed over – provided they are made public in advance.

Note the sympathy afforded to Tony Abbott, who manfully confessed to jumping the wall of his seminary because of uncontrollable lust and then fathering a child on a fellow student, the infant being cast aside for adoption. And compare it with the monstering of Cheryl Kernot, when it was 'revealed' by a breathless Sunday tabloid that she had an affair with a man who had previously been a pupil at a school where she had taught. Recall Bob Hawke's lachrymose confessions of drunkenness and adultery as part of his self-indulgent lifestyle – a lifestyle he continued to pursue to the max right up to the moment he became prime minister and, it now appears, after he left the job. And contrast the general acceptance of Hawke's behaviour with the harassment of Paul Keating over a breach of promise suit brought by a girl named Kristine many years in the past and which was triumphantly unveiled by the opposition as the greatest scandal since – well, since Menzies was sprung in bed with Elizabeth Fairfax, but at least we were able to hush that one up at the time.

By far the best way – indeed the only safe way – to defuse such embarrassments is to make a clean breast of them, while simultaneously putting such a spin on them that they will become a cause for sympathy – even admiration – rather than censure. Do you have a history of congenital insanity? Admit that, from time to time the injustices of the world drive you to despair, but you emerge from such bouts a braver, wiser man, more determined than ever to set things to rights. Did you declare yourself bankrupt after a gambling spree during which you embezzled large sums from your then place of work? Only through such life-changing experiences can one understand the awful complexities of the tax system and need for reform and simplification. Have you been convicted of child molesting? You have? Then for heaven's sake don't tell a soul. In the present climate this is the great unforgivable. It was not always so, and perhaps will not be again some time in the future. But for the moment, there is only one solution: abandon politics and go into the church.

Otherwise your sexuality is hardly a matter of concern. Homosexuals are welcome in the minor parties – well, at least in the Greens and Democrats – and are tolerated in the majors, as long as you don't make a song and dance about it. A touch of sado-masochism is seen as a perfectly acceptable foible, especially the sado bit. Bestiality is best kept to oneself, even in the National Party. If you really must indulge, at least avoid cute and furry endangered species.

So much for preparation; some of it may seem tedious,

but let me assure you it is worthwhile. Without an honest, open, frank and sincere background like the one I have suggested you create, your climb to the top will be that much more difficult. As it will if you don't CHANGE YOUR BLOODY NAME!

Your very, very sincere uncle,
Mungo.

THREE

*In which Terry remains stubborn but
Uncle Mungo makes a persuasive case for change*

My dear Terry – for such you continue, against all my best advice, to call yourself.

I really can't understand your stubborn resistance to the idea of something as simple and painless as a change of name; believe me, if you mean to continue with a career in politics you will have to make far greater personal sacrifices than simply abandoning a worn-out family moniker – although family, honesty and principles are not all that vital to a happy and successful lifestyle either.

If you ever waver in your selfless devotion to the ruthless pursuit of power, always remember that Michael Leunig cartoon in which one of the wretched of the earth is railing at his zillionaire oppressor: 'You have crushed and tormented me, you have stolen my life and hope, you have everything and I have nothing. How do you sleep at night?' To which the rich man replies: 'Actually I sleep between silk sheets on a heated king-size waterbed beside a companion whose beauty would make you weep with desire ...' A reproduction should be in every successful politician's bedroom.

But back to the point. People change their names all the time. Movie stars, pop singers, call girls and others in comparable positions to our own think nothing of it. Even royalty does it: Prince Phillip started out as a minor noble with a string of kraut names like Saxe-Coburg-Hess-Holstein-Brandenburg-Scheisskopf, which was all very well for a European gigolo who just wanted to get into Lizzie's pants, which of course he did, but he never would have ended up as the Duke of bloody Edinburgh without dropping everything except the Brandenburg and anglicising that to Mountbatten. Come to think of it he might have had more fun if he hadn't, but life isn't meant to be fun, at least not when people are watching.

So for the last time: get rid of that tiresome Terry Dobbin and become dashing young Jack Wentworth Bentley. Unless, of course, you have some double game in mind? A subtle plot to lull your rivals into a false sense of security, disregarding you in the belief that no-one with a name like Dobbin could possibly constitute a threat, pursuing their own path towards the top until suddenly you strike like a cobra, like an Exocet missile, like the Battlestar Galactica, reducing them to gibbering impotence, vaporising them to a cloud of quarks …

But no, probably not. At this stage such delights are still beyond you, and perhaps in future I should dictate these missives before lunch. I shall say no more on the subject, except to suggest that no-one with a really wussy name has ever risen beyond a minor ministry, and before you try to get smart, Stanley Bruce wasn't considered wussy in the 1920s and Thatcher was a woman, which made it different.

And please, think of the nicknames. With its carthorse associations, Dobbin positively invites soubriquets like 'Puller' or 'Tugger'. As I think I have already mentioned more than once, your colleagues are quite capable of considerable ingenious cruelty on their own accounts without giving them free kicks.

In the course of his long but ultimately inglorious political career, Andrew Peacock was known first as 'The Colt from Kooyong', a name which at least implied promise, if not achievement. Subsequently this became 'The Show Pony', then 'Gucci' and 'The Sunlamp Kid' – all indicating that the man was style without substance, sizzle without the sausage. Certainly Peacock was one of the vainest men ever to enter parliament; he spent long hours perfecting his tan, insisted on being photographed in left profile and regularly dyed his hair, leading his critics to claim that it had turned prematurely dark with ambition. Paul Keating once greeted his entry to the chamber with the cry: 'Andrew! You've been at the dye pot again!', a remark which was ruled by the speaker to be unparliamentary, but which unquestionably hastened Peacock's eventual demise.

The nicknames became a powerful weapon against him by the forces of his arch-rival John Howard, who suffered only from the appellations 'Honest John' (bestowed for the same reason that red-haired men are called Bluey and dwarves Lofty) and 'Little Johnny' – which his supporters particularly disliked, pointing out repeatedly that Howard was actually taller than the prime minister of the time, Bob Hawke. This was true but irrelevant; the reference had nothing to do with physical height. In private, insiders were less subtle; for some years around Parliament House politicians from all parties referred to Howard simply as 'the little cunt'.

Paul Keating fared only marginally better; in his later years his colleagues christened him 'Captain Wacky'. Hawke himself was known as 'Little Caesar', or 'The Silver Bodgie', neither of which did him much harm. More damaging, superficially at least, were the names given to Howard's hero Sir Robert Menzies by his detractors: 'Pig Iron Bob', for his insistence on shipping iron to pre-war Japan, which of course used it to manufacture weapons used against Australians, and later 'Ming the Merciless', after a cartoon supervillain. Menzies, of course, survived them, as his own mentor, Alfred Deakin, had survived 'Affable Alfred'. But both would probably have preferred to have avoided them altogether, which you just might as Jack Bentley but never will as Terry Dobbin – unless, of course, your colleagues ignore you completely, which would be the only worse fate.

But I have said enough on the subject. I will not add that the issue represents a test of your seriousness in your chosen career, merely that ignoring it would reveal a lack of zeal destined to hobble your ambitions. Horsey – you cannot escape the connection. I can assure you that the cartoonists won't. But enough.

On the subject of cartoonists, it is fortunate that you have no obvious physical characteristic which can be easily exaggerated – not the ears of a Billy McMahon, or the lower lip of a John Howard, to draw on two unfortunate examples. Not that distinctive features are always a disadvantage; John Gorton's rumpled visage worked largely in his favour, although the fact that it was a result of wartime plane crashes obviously helped. (Labor's Mick Young was never convinced. After meeting Gorton's daughter, he insisted that plane crashes were not hereditary. But in the public mind Gorton remained a war hero. Perhaps fortunately, no one mentioned that crashing two planes in a relatively short time might be seen by some as demonstrating a kind of reckless incompetence unsuited to the prime ministership. At least no one did until it was too late.)

And caricature, in politics, is actually more an acknowledgement of success than of contempt; it is far, far better to be ridiculed than ignored, a motto by which both Bronwyn Bishop and her *bête noire*, Bob Ellis, have lived all their lives, thereby achieving a degree of celebrity, if not always admiration. Many politicians demand the originals of the cartoons that mock them most savagely and then display them as proudly as any Anzac Day veteran showing off his war medals. So you need not be afraid that the cartoonists will leave you alone, provided that you gain any position of even quasi-importance in public life. Their job will be to cut you down to size. But it is just as well not to have any physical deformities which will make you look too silly in the process.

However, it may be some years before you become prominent enough for the cartoonists to deign to notice you. In the meantime, strive for a more modest form of recognition. You need some form of personal identity, but not one that is too confronting. Whitlam's immigration minister Al Grassby was certainly noticed, but he would probably have progressed further up the greasy totem pole if he had not insisted on wearing bright purple suits to make sure he stood out in the crowd.

Others have been even more extreme; Bruce Graham from North Sydney arrived in parliament with only one leg and John Hyde from Moore in Western Australia with only one arm, but neither amputation was sufficient to secure elevation

to the ministry. Graham's predecessor, Billy Jack, became famous as a parliamentary mute; in some 17 years in the House of Representatives he asked just eight questions and made seven speeches, one of which was: 'I move that the question be put.' Unsurprisingly, Menzies never offered him preferment, but his constituents loved him; he increased his majority on every election until his retirement, thereby confirming Ben Chifley's adage that more people talk themselves out of parliament than ever talk themselves into it.

There have been those whose careers have been made or broken by a single phrase. Chifley's 'light on the hill' and Menzies' 'forgotten people' have remained in the political vocabulary when many of the real achievements of their originators have been forgotten. Legend has it that the young Doug Anthony took years to live down the phrase he used to introduce himself to his peers: 'I'm a country member.' The only possible reply was: 'Of course we'll remember. How could we ever forget?' And Malcolm Fraser will always be known for his metaphysical pessimism embodied in the phrase: 'Life wasn't meant to be easy.' (And, in spite of what he now claims, he never completed the phrase from George Bernard Shaw: 'But take courage my child, it can be glorious.' If he had, history might recall his prime ministership quite differently.)

Whitlam, in consort with his great speechwriter Graham Freudenberg, coined innumerable *bons mots*, but is best remembered for his speech mannerisms rather than what he actually said; qualifications like 'Compare and contrast', 'Let me put that another way', 'Countries with which we choose to compare ourselves', became essential material for any parodist. But of course Whitlam hardly needed a gimmick to become noticed. His predecessor, Billy McMahon, already conspicuous for his aforementioned ears, also had an unfortunate accent (dubbed by one unkind journalist 'Bhowani Junction chee-chee') in which the liquid consonants L and R turned into the dental plosive D; thus the Canberra suburb of Yarralumla where he lived became Yaddadumda. A naive speechwriter once gave him a sentence to read which began with the word 'militarily'. It came out as something like 'midditiddiddiddee'.

His own predecessor, John Gorton, was as famous for his mangled syntax as for his mangled features and gave his critics many hours of harmless fun as they attempted to deconstruct sentences like his notorious explanation of his proposed health scheme. I have quoted it often in the past, but can't resist the opportunity to give it one more run: 'On the other hand the AMA agrees with us, or, I believe, will agree with us, that it is its policy, and it will be its policy, to inform patients who ask what the common fee is and what our own fee is, so that a patient will know whether he is going to be operated on, if that's what it is, on the basis of the common fee, or not.'

While all of these mannerisms were certainly distinctive, it could be said that they were also distracting; both audiences and the media often paid more attention to them than to the substance of what the various prime ministers were actually saying. In many cases it should be said that this was no bad thing, but a serious propagandist needs his lines to be heard – otherwise what is the point of endlessly repeating them?

And this, of course, is what has to be done if the message,

as it is trendily called, is to get across. The best advice for those aiming to convince the public of something which is against its own interest and/or of dubious value and suspect morality is to keep it simple, say it often and increase your conviction with each repetition. That way there is a good chance that even the most sceptical observer will eventually become so bored and desensitised that he will accept the policy as being irreversible, almost a law of nature; in recent years we have seen this happen with issues such as economic rationalism and globalisation. For a long period these were seen as beyond argument, simply because their proponents had assured us so strenuously and for so long that this was the case, without in fact adducing any real evidence to support it.

Hitler's propaganda chief Josef Goebbels is famous for inventing the concept of the Big Lie; the reasoning was that people might be suspicious of minor deviations from what they knew to be true, but if the new assertion was sufficiently outrageous, they would assume that it could not possibly have been made up. But over the years the Australian experience has shown that a succession of small lies can serve the same purpose, provided only that they become part of a daily ritual.

And it is usually most effective if they are first presented as theories, as alternatives to the currently received wisdom. Thus we start, not with the blanket assertion that all asylum seekers have horns and a tail and have extensive criminal records, suffer from malignant and infectious diseases, deal in drugs and terror and eat their own young, but with the simple suggestion that they are not quite as innocent as they may seem. Then the progression from bludgers and queue jumpers to fiends in human shape can be made in easy stages, each

apparently following logically from the one before. Within a year or two you have a ready-made scapegoat, a threat to the very fabric of Australian society as we know and love it.

Tyros such as yourself are not, of course, in a position to implement such sorcery yet and will not be for some years, but you should certainly recognise it and be ready to take advantage of it when those in higher places wave the wand. In such cases it is always wise to go with the flow; Mr Pickwick had the right approach, as recorded by Charles Dickens: 'It's always best on these occasions to do what the mob do.' 'But suppose there are two mobs?' suggested Mr Snodgrass. 'Shout with the largest,' replied Mr Pickwick. It is no accident that Howard refers affectionately to his supporters as 'the mob' or that many of them have compared him affectionately with the eponymous hero of *The Pickwick Papers*. They weren't just talking about his appearance.

For the aspiring politician the message is simple: if you sense a passing bandwagon, leap aboard. To attempt to stand against the attacks of mass hysteria that periodically descend on Australian politics is simply foolhardy. There is little satisfaction in knowing your position is the reasonable, honest and correct one if you don't have the numbers to enforce it. Examples of such Quixotism go back a long way. Ada Holman, the wife of a New South Wales premier in the early twentieth century, described a memorable instance in her memoirs: 'If ever oratory could convince it should have done so by the most stirring speech surely ever made in the parliament of New South Wales. Mr W.M. Hughes spoke against Australia sending a contingent to fight against the Boers. W.A. Holman was admittedly a finer orator than W.M. but he himself always declared that Hughes' speech on this occasion was unsurpass-able. "It reached the heights of the sublime," was my husband's verdict. "Not Burke, nor Grattan, nor Gladstone, nor O'Con-nell, nor any of the magicians of the spoken word ever got near its magnificence." I sat in the speaker's gallery throughout the night and heard the three-hour speech. It was nearly mid-night when Hughes got a hearing but time stood still while the magic words came pouring out from seemingly inex-haustible depths. The speaker was by times passionate, by times logical, presenting the situation of the heroic Boers with irresistible force, by times witty, tearing the racketeers to bits with biting rancour, scathingly cutting up their patriotism which evinced itself by crushing a small nation to death for the possession of its gold. "He's got them now, he's got them!" I reflected as cheer after cheer went up from the throats of opponents, as tears ran down the hardened cheeks, as breath-less silence followed every syllable. "How right he is," a bitter antagonist of Hughes said to me. "How unanswerably right!" When the division was taken about 3.00am Hughes had secured seven votes in a house crowded to capacity. So much for oratory, so much for the right, when party is at stake.'

Read, mark, learn and inwardly digest, young aspirant. Many an opponent of the war in Vietnam suffered the same fate. They were, of course, right, and their viewpoint was eventually vindicated. But that didn't prevent them being reviled across the political spectrum as cowards and traitors at the time, and even when the whole Vietnam adventure was seen to have been at best a costly mistake, those who had warned against it in the first place received little or no public credit. Bringers of bad, or still worse unpopular, news seldom do.

But by and large the mob looks after its own, as was proved in the earlier-mentioned case of the asylum seekers. Even after it was conclusively shown that Howard and his ministers had lied in their neatly capped teeth about children being thrown overboard and children having their lips sewn together, it made no discernible difference to the mob's view of the situation. The general view was that even if the heathen devils were innocent of these specific atrocities, they were still guilty of unspeakable crimes – so unspeakable, in fact, that no one could even attempt to tell you what they were.

You see the trick: first convince the public that the group involved are criminals, and then by definition the evils that can be attributed to them are limited only by your own imagination. Tell the people what they want to hear: this is the secret of great demagoguery. It need hardly be added (but I will make one final plea): they will believe it all the more readily if it comes from someone with a fine, honest, no-nonsense name like Jack Bentley.

Regards from your still hopeful uncle,
Mungo.

FOUR

*In which Terry succumbs and a delighted
Uncle Mungo points the way to future imposture*

My Dear Jack – my Dear Jack Wentworth Bentley!!!

I need hardly tell you how delighted I am that you have finally taken the plunge. The fact that it had more to do with your desire to avoid a particularly importunate creditor and an enraged husband than with naked political ambition matters not a jot. The point is that you have accepted one of the most fundamental tenets of your new career: if you are to succeed in the noble aim of putting your ideas into place it can only be done by achieving a position of power, and in an imperfect world this in turn may necessitate the odd trifling compromise with an absurdly strict code of ethics.

Or, as the Jesuits might put it more crudely, the end justifies the means – not always, of course, but in this case your departure from absolute truth and righteousness is too trivial to count. It's not as if we're asking you to sacrifice one of your children. Not yet, anyway.

Having taken this first step, you will find that the peccadilloes, little white lies and minor acts of betrayal which are so much part of the job, will come more easily as time goes on. Think of it not as the first step down the slippery slope but the first hike up the greasy totem pole. Think of it as forward, ever forward, not a backward step, face towards the foe, excelsior and all that crap. I'll bet you feel better already.

And of course there will be immediate, tangible benefits. Think only of possibilities the name Bentley opens up for campaign slogans. Bentley – on the move. Bentley puts you in the driver's seat. I can rely on my Bentley, because Bentley never stalls. Bentley gives you fingertip control. And about the worst easy retort is the tagline from an old radio show: Gently, Bentley.

Slogans, incidentally, can be tricky things. Ideally, a good slogan contains the name of the candidate (it is surprising how few voters can recall this without aid) and is usually in rhyming form to drive the message home. For some reason this appears especially necessary in Queensland. The re-doubtable Russ Hinze, the 130-kilogram transport minister christened 'The Colossus of Roads', used to rely on the simple: 'Don't fuss, Vote Russ', which sent even his older con-stituents scanning their ballot papers each election for a candidate named Mr Russ. A Labor man, Eddie Foat, used a multi-coloured poster with the line 'Don't miss the boat vote Foat', reinforced by an illustration of the candidate's head protruding from the funnel of a ferry. A National Party rival fell back on 'Keep Shoutin' Vote Houghton', which confused an electorate more used to rhyming his name with rortin'.

Labor veteran Fred Daly decided to abandon straight rhyme for wordplay: on one occasion he went biblical with the exhortation: 'Give us this day our Daly Fred'. His oppo-nent came back with: 'Keep yourself nice; change Daly'. Fortunately for Fred they didn't.

Slogans without rhymes (or even those with) should be checked and rechecked for the opportunities they offer graffitists. An otherwise sensible Liberal once spent a lot of money on bumper stickers proclaiming, 'Haslem's a hit!' to which his opponents had to add but a single letter to render the exercise counterproductive. At least the all-purpose: 'Bloggs – working for the electorate' requires the alteration of two characters to reverse its intent.

Let it merely be said that while few careers have been made purely by the right slogan, more than a few have been largely unmade by the wrong one. American presidential campaigns are instructive. In 1964 the conservative Republican Barry Goldwater tried to overcome the impression that he was too reactionary for the electorate by running under the line: 'In your heart you know he's right'. The Democrats immediately replied: 'In your guts you know he's nuts', and LBJ won in a landslide. And in 1960 Richard Nixon never lived down his opponents' challenge: 'Would you buy a used car from this man?'

However, all this is still in front of you; at this stage you do not even have preselection. And there is no time to lose in lining it up. But first, decide for which seat you are aiming. The instinct, of course, is to go for a reasonably safe one; to target an electorate where the sitting member is getting fairly long in the tooth and perhaps can be talked into an early retirement (if you have any friends in business who can bribe him or her with the promise of a lucrative sinecure, so much the better); or, failing that, to look for a seat where the sitting member has grown lazy and unpopular and, with the aid of a little judicious branch stacking, may therefore be vulnerable to a challenge.

But of course, many of your fellow aspirants will have had

the same idea and may have been diligently white-anting their representative for some time. Such targets are so obvious to the ambitious that a newcomer will seldom get a clear run at them and may in fact be savaged so severely that his progress up the greasy totem pole may be set back by years if he tries for one. Moreover, head office often has its own plans for them – you are not yet ready to tackle the local equivalent of Tammany Hall.

So lower your sights a fraction. Look for a seat which is not yet safe, perhaps not yet even marginal, but is heading in that direction. Study its record in the last few elections: is there a clear trend one way or another? Has it defied national swings? If so, do the demographics of the area suggest that this tendency will continue, even accelerate? Or is it due to some exceptional circumstance – a series of unpopular decisions which have alienated a group of usually reliable voters, who may, nonetheless, just as easily be bribed back to the fold next time around.

And check out the incumbent member, be he or she friend or foe. Do not be fooled by appearances. I have already mentioned the notorious member for North Sydney, 'Silent' Billy Jack. In Canberra Jack never did anything even remotely noteworthy; indeed, except on the rare occasions when his vote was needed in close divisions, he need not have bothered turning up and may not have – few if any would have noticed his absence. But in his own electorate he worked tirelessly to satisfy his constituents' complaints about garbage collections, the siting of bus stops, the delivery of newspapers – no cause was too silly or trivial for Jack, despite the fact that practically none of the queries he answered came under the purview of the federal government. Others would have fobbed them off to the local state member or the council; Jack took them all on board. No plaintive cat was ever stranded up a tree while he was the local member.

Standards may have changed in modern times, but it is still a truism of politics that no matter how incompetent, stupid or even corrupt politicians may become, the ones that look after their grass-roots base are bloody hard to shift. Even so it can be done, because another truism is that self-interest, if sufficiently ruthless, will generally prevail. Bribery, threats and blackmail are technically illegal, but all have a place in a hard-fought preselection battle. To those who object to such tactics on legal and ethical grounds, or simply as a matter of personal taste, the invariable reply is: 'If you can't stand the heat, get out of the kitchen.' Preselections, like nature, are usually red in tooth and claw and definitely not for the squeamish.

Branch stacking, however, in spite of what you have read in the newspapers, is not illegal. In a vague sort of way it is against party rules, but the rules are so ill drawn that any half-smart bush lawyer could drive a horse and cart through them. Not that this will necessarily help in the long run, because in case of dispute the final say is with the party head office, which does not usually feel itself bound by any law of man, God or nature. But it is nice to know that branch stacking is not, in itself, a criminal offence. You will probably have to commit a few of these during your political career, but it is best to keep the list as short as possible.

But wait. What is a criminal offence is giving false information to the Commonwealth Electoral Office, and this includes enrolling yourself or any of your friends and acquaintances at a false address. It should be noted at once that this is only a problem in the Labor Party, because only the Labor Party insists that members who vote in preselections actually have a place of residence inside the electorate. To the more globally minded Liberals such limitations are considered unnecessarily restrictive. Anyone can join any branch that takes their fancy. To vote for your favourite candidate it is not essential to live in the same area, the same state or even the same country. In one celebrated instance in the Queensland electorate of Ryan a preselection hopeful named Michael Johnson received a number of votes from supporters in Hong Kong, many of whom had never set foot in Australia. Party headquarters eventually decided that this was going a bit far, but still stopped short of demanding local residence as a qualification.

Thus Liberals will never be hauled before the courts over the rorting of preselections while their more scrupulous Labor opponents, who use the Electoral Roll to check eligibility, quite frequently are, and become the object of thundering denunciations from the pious conservatives. It is a wonderful example of vice being its own political reward, a concept with which you will become more familiar over time.

So: for the Labor Party, branch stacking, while not a crime in itself, may involve the commission of a crime to make it work. However, if you are reasonably subtle about it you can usually ensure that no-one springs you until it is too late. Even in the face of conclusive evidence, parties are invariably reluctant to reverse a *fait accompli*. One way out, of course, is to ensure that all your stackees actually do live in the

electorate. There is no need to waste time explaining the situation to them: simply go to your local pub around closing time with a stack of membership forms, and intone the mantra: 'Name and address and sign here, and the beer's on me.' Then discard those from outside the boundaries.

If you actually plan to enrol them at false addresses, then more finesse is needed. It is generally a mistake to enrol more than ten people in the same one-bedroom flat; questions may be asked. Also, try to be discreet about the mixture of people you enrol; your colleagues may look askance if you introduce an entire ethnic football club into the branch on the same night. But with care and over a period, you may be able to secure the numbers.

Even then, others may try to subvert them. One of the problems of preselection votes is that they are generally done by secret ballot. Thus it is difficult to know which of your hard-won stackees are honest enough to have stayed bought. As numerous politicians have found over centuries, treachery is rife, and a direct approach seldom works.

Suppose you ask one of your colleagues point-blank for his or her vote. The reply: 'Well, you're obviously the outstanding candidate' means: I won't vote for you. 'There's no doubt you deserve the seat' means: I won't vote for you. 'At this stage you're certainly top of my list' means: I won't vote for you. 'Of course I owe you much more than just a vote' means: I won't vote for you. 'Of course you know you can count on my vote' means: I just might vote for you. 'I've always been part of your team' means: I'll probably vote for you unless I get a better offer. 'Look. I'll stand next to your best mate Fred, and I'll even show him my ballot paper before

I hand it in' means: Either both Fred and I will vote for you or neither of us will.

This last 'show and tell' method, incidentally, used to be popular with the Labor Party factions during caucus room ballots. The late, great numbers man Pat Kenneally insisted that his troops use it during the take-no-prisoners battles of the 1950s. If he was really dubious about how one of them might vote, he surreptitiously put a pinprick in a corner of the man's ballot paper as they were distributed, and watched for it to turn up during the count. More than one turncoat was unmasked by this tactic.

The obvious lesson here is that, no matter how thoroughly you think you might have tied up the numbers, the vote's never over until it is actually counted. It is amazing how many otherwise rational politicians forget this in the heat of battle, and express surprise, stupefaction, even moral outrage, when they find they have been dudded. When Bob Hawke finally decided to take the plunge and enter parliament it was in the wake if a huge row with the then party leader, Bill Hayden, at the Adelaide federal conference. Hawke found himself outmanoeuvred by Hayden during a vote on industrial policy, and was so distressed that he spent the next 24 hours drinking. This in itself was hardly unusual, but his later outburst to a group of journalists: 'As far as Bill Hayden and I are concerned, it's finished. Bill Hayden is a lying cunt with a limited future,' was considered a trifle excessive.

Even then he didn't learn; after Hayden beat off his first leadership challenge, Hawke complained aggrievedly to anyone who would listen that there were a lot of fucking liars in the caucus; why, a clear fucking majority had said they would fucking vote for him. Maybe they had – once; but that is never a guarantee. A vote is a tender plant; it needs to be tended, fed and watered, cozened and schmoozed. And even then some other bastard might come along and harvest it behind your back. Take nothing for granted, even when – especially when – you appear most secure.

In this regard it is always best to have a trusted colleague (well, insofar as any colleague can be trusted) who is able and willing to watch your back and warn you in advance of impending defections. Most such eventually turn on their masters demanding their own turn at the top, but for a time at least they will be your most valuable possession, a sort of political American Express card (don't leave caucus without it).

If you ever make it to the leadership, such a deputy is beyond price. In recent years only one man has genuinely filled the office: Labor's Lance Barnard, who, when offered the crown himself as a compromise between the factions of Gough Whitlam and Jim Cairns, declined it and remained loyal to Whitlam, the bloody fool. The mere fact that he was prepared to sacrifice his own ambition for what he saw as the good of the party forever disqualified him from a leadership role. All others have seen the job in terms of self-advantage and bugger the elected leader. Phil Lynch deserted Bill Snedden for Malcolm Fraser; Lionel Bowen dropped Hayden for Hawke. John Howard spent his entire time as deputy undermining Andrew Peacock, and was appalled when his own deputy Fred Chaney ratted to return to Peacock. Peter Reith only ever saw John Hewson as a stepping-stone to be surmounted. Paul Keating saw it as only natural that he should push Hawke aside when his turn came, and Peter Costello is rapidly coming to the same conclusion about Howard.

Remember always: there are no true friendships in politics except among the failures. Life at the top depends on a series of shifting alliances, and the best way to detect the shifts before they actually happen is through your own network of spies and enforcers, who may be vicious and crazy, but will never try to knock you off. The great Indian prime minister Jawaharlal Nehru once remarked to Ben Chifley how valuable it was to have loyal allies to back him up when he was right. The practical Chifley replied: 'Even more valuable when you happen to be wrong.' The best place to recruit such devotees is among rank outsiders, newcomers to the House of Representatives who have not yet gained the clout to become a threat, or senators trapped in the upper house and therefore unable to make an overt bid for the top job.

This, of course, is why Senator Bill Heffernan has played such an important role in maintaining John Howard in the top job and will continue to do so. He has nowhere else to go; even before his baseless accusations against Judge Michael Kirby he was regarded as a raving loony, a political accident waiting to happen, and these days he is so hopelessly compromised that no one but Howard is thick-skinned enough to be in the same office as him. He is bound to Howard with hoops of steel, and is therefore a willing purveyor of whatever malignity Howard and his brains trust can dream up. I am not suggesting you are likely to find anyone so disgustingly effective, even if you reach the summit; few have purged themselves so thoroughly of everyday standards of decency as has Howard, and he is of course to be admired for it, even if not always emulated.

But it is time to start gathering a team of informers and enforcers around you. Even if you cannot promise them the paradisiacal rewards with which the chief of the assassins, the Old Man of the Mountain Hasan Sabbah, tantalised his drug-addled followers, there is at least the prospect – no, now that you have taken that crucial first step, the certainty, I feel it in my bones – of power, the ultimate aphrodisiac, the true nectar of the megalomaniac. Or, as Labor's head kicker Graham Richardson once put it rather more prosaically, better than sex and almost as good as a really good feed.

Stay hungry, my dear Jack Wentworth Bentley, and again congratulations from your delighted uncle,

Mungo.

FIVE

*In which we learn to fabricate sincerity,
feign veracity and counterfeit charm*

My Dear Jack – My, how quickly that name develops a familiarity. It's almost as if you were born with it.

And now you are settling into your new nomenclature, it's time to develop a *persona* to go with it. By *persona* I don't just mean a plausible and attractive *curriculum vitae* – we have already dealt with that. Nor am I referring merely to the superficial mannerisms by which you will be judged on television. There is plenty of time for you to find the appropriate professional coach to train you in the art of the spontaneous gesture and the frank and open approach. This is not nearly as hard as it may sound and is in fact the basis from which all other simulation flows; as an actress whose name I now forget (but was clearly a loss to politics) once said, if you can fake sincerity you can fake anything. And you will of course be an achingly sincere politician.

But we now have to decide just what sort of sincere politician you should become. Should you attempt bluff, hearty populism in the manner of Bob Hawke? A more distant but always commanding presence in the style of Malcolm Fraser? Or perhaps the exciting and dangerous approach of Paul Keating? The quick answer to this is: none of the above. Imitation may be the sincerest form of flattery, but in politics it invariably fails because it inevitably falls short of the original. The politician who tries to ape his rival or predecessor is, almost by definition, a second rater, inferior to the real thing.

In a slightly different context this explains the downfall of Kim Beazley in 2001. Having decided, wrongly, that the GST was the real issue, he decided to avoid distracting attention from it by agreeing with John Howard about everything else – up to and including the treatment of asylum seekers. Faced with what was really no choice at all, people decided they might as well vote for the leader who devised the policies rather than the follower who just went along with them – for the organ grinder rather than the monkey.

It certainly does no harm to study the successful techniques of others and to adapt the best bits to your own advantage, but under no circumstances try to make yourself into a cardboard replica of one of the greats. Be yourself – 'this above all: to thine own self be true and it must follow as the night the day thou canst not then be false to any man.' Of course silly old Polonius got it wrong: you will indeed be false to quite a lot of people over the years, and do so with gusto and panache. But it is important to carve out your own niche first.

Keating himself realised this at a young age: after one of his rousing performances as a fresh young member of parliament, Gough Whitlam himself offered his congratulations. 'That was a good speech,' intoned the great leader. 'You should go back to the university, comrade, and get yourself an honours degree.' Keating rejected what he saw as patronising advice with contempt. 'What for? Then I'd be like you,' he retorted. Given that the aim of most young Laborites was to become as close to Whitlam as possible, this seemed both silly and arrogant. But Keating was right: to succeed he needed to be Paul Keating writ large, not Gough Whitlam writ small.

He did, however, have a somewhat unlikely hall of heroes of his own. Chief among them was one of Labor's more reviled figures, Jack Lang, who ratted on the party after having been sacked as New South Wales premier by Governor Sir Philip Game. (Incidentally, notice how the name Jack keeps recurring in these missives? It must be a good omen.) Lang was a bitter man, an authoritarian, a racist and above all a great hater. But Keating sat at his feet and learned Labor history from him, and eventually campaigned successfully to have him readmitted to the party shortly before his death. Keating's other mentor was Whitlam's resources minister Rex Connor, another big man whose over-stretched ambitions led to the disastrous loans affair and, after Whitlam sacked him from the ministry for disobeying a cabinet instruction and misleading parliament, to the blocking of supply and the dismissal of the Whitlam government.

At first glance the two seem just about the worst role models it is possible to imagine. But both were tough guys, the kind who slapped their opponents around without mercy. Lang was known as 'The Big Fella' and Connor as 'The Strangler'. It was probably their ability to inspire fear rather than the wisdom of their policies and the subtlety of their political strategy that made them attractive to Keating, and how well he learned the lesson.

Others have had almost equally bizarre idols. When Billy Snedden became treasurer, he was asked which of his predecessors in the job he would most like to emulate. To the

surprise of his audience, the former Melbourne newsboy
nominated Alfred Deakin and King O'Malley. The choice was
particularly baffling as neither man had in fact been a treasurer: Deakin was three times prime minister and also held the
external affairs portfolio and O'Malley had twice been minister for home affairs before the portfolio was abolished, but
that was it. However, as the careers of both men began and
ended in the first few years after federation, none of the journalists present realised the error. Some did, however, recall that
both Deakin and O'Malley had been a trifle eccentric. Deakin
believed he communed with the spirits of long-dead politicians who instructed him on both policy and tactics;
O'Malley's enthusiasms led to almost incomprehensibly florid
language, as with the establishment of the Commonwealth
Bank: 'Its importance is so overpowering that I tremble. Hope
sees a star and listening love hears the rustle of a wing.' In the
circumstances Snedden's stint as treasurer was quite remarkably pedestrian.

Bob Hawke acknowledged no superiors, but accepted
that John Curtin was the greatest of his predecessors. The fact
that both men had to promise to reform their drinking before
their colleagues would grant them the leadership may have
had something to do with this. But there was no denying his
hunger for recognition.

Hawke's method of winning people over was to sum up
their interests at a glance and then convince them that, whatever their speciality, he was on top of it. Fellow politicians
received an instant dissertation on the state of the nation. Pub-
licans were treated to a critical analysis on the quality of their
beer. Sporty types got a lecture on football tactics and, if they

were lucky, a tip for the races. At our first meeting he instantly tabbed me as an arty-crafty and hit me with a lengthy quotation from Shakespeare. Amused, I wrote a short piece about his chameleon-like qualities. When we next crossed paths his greeting was more abrupt: 'Thanks, cunt,' he rasped.

But Hawke made a lasting political reputation on the basis of consensus, of appealing to everyone; with typical immodesty he described it as his never-ending love affair with the Australian people. The fastidious would say this was going too far: for real politicians the people aren't there to be loved, they are there to be cajoled, bribed, bullied, manipulated – whatever it takes to get their vote. But if you can persuade the mob, as Howard (remember) calls his followers, that you really, really respect them while at the same time retaining a Mark Anthony-like disdain, then, my dear Jack, you are well on your way.

I should add that one attribute almost all truly successful politicians have is the ability to charm the knickers off a nun. The only exceptions in my lifetime to this rule have been Billy McMahon (who should probably not be described as a successful politician anyway) and perhaps Malcolm Fraser, whose patrician aloofness never let up sufficiently for even those closest to him to feel comfortable (his playful habit of slipping pickled onions into their pockets in the members' bar obviously didn't help either). But the others – Menzies, Holt, Gorton, Whitlam, Hawke, Keating, and even Howard on a good day – have all had their respective followers eating out of their hands when the occasion arose. It is true that this was seldom if ever the way the general public saw them, which is as it should be; there are few occasions when the head of government needs to waste his precious charm on the *hoi polloi*. But when it comes to winning over individuals for vital votes, to seducing media commentators into supporting your point of view, to persuading former mistresses not to go running to Harry M. Miller with their stories – ah, that's when charm becomes important. Cultivate it; like all the semblances needed by a politician, it can be acquired by diligent practice.

And while we're at it, learn to play tennis. This is a most useful hobby for a politician; even a few practice swings can give the impression of boundless energy, and you can sit down again as soon as the television cameras have left. It is a good middle-of-the-road sport; not rich and snobby like polo or identifiably working class like racing greyhounds. It has a clean and wholesome image without being in any way priggish. If you have only one outside interest (and arguably you should have a couple – the study of a particular branch of history always sounds good, and no one is going to test you if you stay away from trivia nights) then tennis is the way to go.

If tennis is just too strenuous for your overworked body, then try an indoor sport such as snooker, a popular pastime among politicians after the house rises. It can give your career a welcome boost. Jim Cope, a long-serving member of no discernible achievement, was elected speaker by his Labor colleagues largely on the strength of his long reign as undisputed snooker champion of Parliament House.

Dress, of course, should be neat but casual. The dark double-breasted suit which was entirely appropriate to the Menzies era now appears pompous and old-fashioned, which is probably why John Howard still frequently affects it. It is still worth having your clothes made to measure – this implies a

concern with appearances still demanded by the more conservative voters – but there is no need to go to the lengths of Paul Keating, whose Italian look was both expensive and pretentious. In any case, most of the mob wouldn't recognise an Armani if they were in bed with it.

Avoid, at all costs, dressing up if circumstances demand you visit rural areas, an exercise which is best avoided in any case. There is nothing sillier than the sight of a citified politician dollied up in brand-new moleskins, Driza-Bone and Akubra. John Howard's earnest attempts to win the bush in rustic headgear reminded viewers not of a hardy pioneer, but of a roofing nail.

Still worse is the idea of donning fancy dress when attending ethnic functions. Not only will you look ridiculous; you are almost certain to get some important detail wrong, thereby starting a blood feud which will endure for centuries. It is, however, worth learning a greeting in the language involved, as long as you are very, very careful to get it exactly right. A minor mistake in intonation, or even a misplaced word, can be disastrous, as even the greatest and most powerful have discovered. When American president John F. Kennedy visited Berlin during the blockade, he sought to express his solidarity with the citizens by telling them: 'I am a Berliner.' Unfortunately he inserted the definite article: instead of 'Ich bin Berliner,' he boasted: 'Ich bin ein Berliner,' meaning, in the local vernacular, 'I am a doughnut.' Thousands of would-be presidents have woken screaming from nightmares in which they did the same.

Language can be a problem in other ways. I have seldom seen it reported, but politicians as a class are among the most foul-mouthed people in the country – in private, of course, or at least in what they think is private. Their intimate conversations are a constant stream of obscenity. This is something to which you will have to grow accustomed, or else risk being dismissed as a wowser and a wimp. Swearing is a mark of toughness, of the killer instinct now demanded from any political aspirant who wishes to be taken seriously. This applies to women as well as to men, to those professing deep religious principles as well as to hardened atheists. The New South Wales Labor Right is notoriously dominated by (allegedly) devout Roman Catholics, but its meetings consist almost entirely of (expletive deleted)s.

This does no real harm when it is kept behind closed doors, but there is always the risk that an excitable politician will absent-mindedly carry the same practice into the public arena. Worse still, of course, is the prospect of getting sprung during what is intended to be a free and frank exchange of views between colleagues. This is what happened to Andrew Peacock and Victorian Premier Jeff Kennett after the latter had returned from a run-in with John Howard and fortified himself with a few stiff drinks. Kennett then rang Peacock to tell him about it, but their mobile phone conversation was intercepted and a bowdlerised version of it published in the Melbourne press. One actual exchange went like this. Kennett: 'I said, I couldn't give a fuck. I've got no sympathies anymore. You're all a pile of shit. And tomorrow I'm going berserk. Well, he went off his brain, and at the end of it I said to him: Howard, you're a cunt, you haven't got my support, you never will have. And I'm not going to rubbish you or the party tomorrow but I feel a lot better having told you you're a cunt. And the poor little fellow didn't know whether he was Arthur or Martha.' Peacock: 'Well fuck him. I'm not worried. I almost bloody cried. My fucking anger yesterday as Margaret knows ... The first thing I came in last night I said, aah, fucking cunts! I said the whole fucking thing could upset tomorrow, and she said What's Jeffrey done, and I said, it's not what Jeffrey's done, it's what everyone's fucking done to Jeffrey ...'

Unsurprisingly, Peacock was asked to resign from Howard's front bench and Kennett and Howard played no speaks for some weeks. But the public damage done to Peacock, in particular, was more lasting. The incident allowed Howard (who, incidentally, can coin a neat expletive or two when he chooses) to take the high moral ground and dismiss Peacock as a ratbag. This, of course, made it all the more galling when the party, in a spectacular lapse of judgement, dropped him and reinstated Peacock as leader a couple of years later.

The undisputed master of the scabrous insult was Paul Keating, but even his opponents had to admit that Keating's delivery, while undoubtedly coarse, often had a certain style and even wit. At some later date I shall send you a representative collection of great political put-downs to study and possibly emulate, but for the moment it should suffice to list some of the epithets he bestowed on the opposition from time to time: harlots, sleazebags, frauds, immoral cheats, blackguards, pigs, mugs, clowns, boxheads, criminal intellects, criminals, stupid crooks, corporate crooks, friends of tax cheats, brain-damaged, loopy crims, stupid foul-mouthed grub, piece of criminal garbage, dullards, stupid, mindless, crazy, alley cat, bunyip aristocracy, clot, fop, gigolo, hare-brained hillbilly, malcontent, mealy-mouthed, ninny, rustbucket, scumbag, scum, sucker, thug, dimwits, dummies, a swill, a pig sty, Liberal muck, vile constituency, fools and incompetents, rip-off merchants, perfumed gigolos, gutless spiv, glib rubbish, tripe and drivel, constitutional vandals, stunned mullets, half-baked crim, insane stupidities, champion liar, ghouls of the national party, barnyard bullies, piece of parliamentary filth. And that was on the floor of the parliament alone – in private he could really be quite rude.

I do not suggest you go down this track, at least not yet. But from the very beginning you can start working on your potential rivals. At this stage it should be enough to suggest that they are a bit casual in their approach to politics, part-timers and amateurs, dilettantes who are not really serious. To the professionals who run the parties these days, such accusations amount to almost automatic disqualification. Contrast your own willingness to throw yourself body and soul into the fray, to put all your time and energy at the service of the party, irrespective of personal cost. (See? Already the name change, which we understand was done for purely selfish reasons, can be parleyed into a political plus.)

Don't take it too far; your superiors are by definition politicians, having moved themselves up the ladder by similar tactics, and will no doubt recognise this for the bullshit that it is. But they will also recognise one of their own, someone who is indeed serious about clawing his way onward, who is already learning and experimenting with the elementary techniques of kicking and gouging. As long as you make it clear that you are no threat to their own advancement – at least not yet – they are unlikely to reject someone they may well be able to use to their own advantage.

A final tip: during the ascent of the greasy totem pole you will undoubtedly change in many ways. By the end of the process you will not recognise yourself. But don't try to do it all at once; wait until the need arises. A good example is your voice. I hate to mention it, but most of the time you sound like an adenoidal homosexual. This is a disadvantage, but not a fatal one: we have already noted Billy McMahon's chee chee accent, and could add Alexander Downer's plumminess, Bob Hawke's gurgling rasp, Kim Beazley's impression of an attenuated theremin and John Howard's constant whingeing squawk to those who have made it without sounding like Menzies, Bob Carr or Don Dunstan – all of whom had voices that radio advertisers of sanitary products would have killed for. You will probably find that time and practice modulate your vocal eccentricities; but if they don't, just live with them. At least they are distinctive.

Do not, under any circumstances, attempt voice training. Bill Hayden did, and perhaps partly as a result of his deafness, became even more incomprehensible as a result. And of course, the word might get out. There was a time when listeners to the BBC were treated to a pirated tape of Margaret Thatcher rehearsing the phrase 'Enough is enough' over and over again with the aid of a famous actor. Even in England, the Iron Lady barely survived the ridicule that followed. In Australia, you wouldn't have a hope.

The same of course applies to appearance. A little modification such as hairstyling and dyeing, eyebrow plucking and tooth capping is now quite acceptable; one current member –

Brendan Nelson – has even been known to sport an earring. And in this context I should probably mention the need to avoid transvestism. You probably find such a warning both unnecessary and offensive, but since Alexander Downer's appearance in fishnet stockings the boundaries of credulity have been stretched to breaking point. On the whole it is better not to tinker with what nature has provided, basic though it is. Your public will grow used to you, and all the more as your character shines through, reshaping the outer man as it does so – the character, of course, being that of Jack Wentworth Bentley, to whom I send my best wishes for the sincerest of transformations.

Your uncle,
Mungo.

SIX

*In which Uncle Mungo advises on
cozening the loathsome electorate*

MASTER THE LANGUAGE

My Dear Jack,

Until now we have generally discussed the brighter side of politics – gigantic personal ambition amounting to a form of megalomania and the fun one can have realising it, through larks such as deception, treachery and the like. But it is time to warn you that there is a dark side to the great game too, an aspect which is no fun at all.

The worst thing about politics can be summed up in a single word: voters. Without the electorate, life would be so much easier. Politicians could compete on something approaching the level playing field so beloved of economic fundamentalists and their fellow necromancers, secure in the knowledge that the rules (or rather, the lack of them) applied equally to all, that the game was an end in itself unsullied by distractions from the world outside. But alas, reality is crueller and more complex. Before being allowed to pass go and collect the gigantic rewards, both financial and otherwise, which are available to the best of the players, you must perform the political equivalent of throwing a six, and you must be prepared to repeat the process at least once every three years.

The problem, of course, is getting elected to a seat and then holding on to it. We have already discussed, in broad terms,

75

getting preselection; the compromises, deals and occasional fraud and criminality that are entailed. But this is only the start, even in seats which are generally considered safe. In these troubled times even the bluest of blue-ribbon constituencies have been known to spawn loathsome independents, some of whom (in rural areas at least) have actually knocked off long-standing sitting members, or weakened their grip to such an extent that their progress up the greasy totem poll has been stalled, or even permanently halted.

I have already mentioned the case of Bronwyn Bishop and Bob Ellis: the latter stood against the former in what should have been the rock-solid Liberal seat of Mackellar on Sydney's northern beaches. Bishop was at that stage playing for very high stakes indeed, or at least believed that she was; it was the time of maximum instability in the parliamentary party and the quest for a messiah with the popular appeal to drag the coalition back to the treasury benches was at its most desperate. Somehow the diminutive figure of Bishop, raised to a respectable height only by a more than usually unfriendly hairdo, moved abruptly from the sillier gossip columns into the sillier political columns and the whispers of her ambitions for the top job became – in the tabloids at least – positive roars.

In retrospect, the idea was as ridiculous as the mad quest for Canberra some years before by Queensland Premier Joh Bjelke-Petersen; despite all the puffery from fans in the popular media, neither aspirant ever had more than a handful of votes in the party room, which is where leaders actually have to be elected, even in the conservative groupings. (The good old days when leaders were supposed to emerge, fully armed, from the body of the party without the need for any form of democratic process, even the limited vote allowed by such revolutionary organisations as the Catholic College of Cardinals, are, alas, long gone.) So Bishop was always a phantom menace rather than a real one, but this did not limit her public exposure – indeed, if anything it enhanced it.

Appalled by the prospect, and also, it must be admitted, attracted by the prospect of near-limitless publicity, the scruffy figure of Ellis, a long-time Labor fellow-traveller, announced that he would stand against her at the by-election in which, by what should have been a formality, she planned to transfer from the senate to a safe house of representatives seat as a necessary step towards the leadership. The ALP wisely declined to stand a candidate, leaving the field to Ellis, and with the aid of the theatrical push living in and around the area he gave it an almighty shake; there was a substantial anti-Liberal swing, and although Bishop clawed her way into the seat her alleged popularity with the electorate – the only thing she had going for her as a qualification for the top job – was irrevocably damaged. Of course, she would never have made it even if Ellis had not stood against her, but she may have remained some kind of a force in the party, at least a focus for discontent. As it was she sank steadily into a well-merited obscurity.

I am not suggesting that you would ever be as absurd a figure as Bronwyn Bishop (for a start, you lack the coiffure) but beware, always beware, of a popular independent ambushing you in these volatile times. Like other terrorists, they are hard to detect and even harder to kill off.

But even if you escape this threat, the electorate will take up an unconscionable amount of your time. Perhaps the most damaging accusation that can be made against a politician – certainly against a backbencher, which you will inevitably be for quite a while – is that of 'neglecting the electorate'. An electorate spurned is a very dangerous political beast; it can turn unpredictably and savage the master at whose feet it has lain, uncomplainingly, for many years.

Take the case of the veteran National Party MP Ian Sinclair, for decades a minister and one stage the actual party leader: having finally decided to resign from his seat of New England he changed his mind at the last minute, and fronted his party branch to demand reinstatement. After hearing him out, the chairman asked him politely what he had done for the electorate recently. 'Well,' replied Sinclair, 'I got you the New England Highway' – and indeed he did; in an extraordinary exercise in pork barrelling Sinclair, as minister for transport, had designated the New England, rather than the much more trafficked Pacific, as the main route between Sydney and Brisbane and consequently as the recipient of Commonwealth funding. The chairman nodded. 'But Ian,' he said gently, 'that was 30 years ago' – and indeed it was. Even for the patient squatters of the northern tablelands, 30 years is a long time between drinks. Sinclair's bid failed.

You will not, of course, be expected to deliver a super-highway to your electorate every few years – even in the most marginal seat the voters are not quite so unreasonable. But you will be expected to be visible, interested, caring and sharing. One old-fashioned Labor man summed it up by saying: 'All the electorate wants is a good fuck every couple of months, and even the laziest member ought to be up to that.' But it is really even easier and requires no Viagra;

the voters just want to be noticed. With some justification, they feel that this is not too much to ask in exchange for keeping you in the lifestyle to which you desperately want to become accustomed.

The problem is that they don't just want to be noticed *en masse*; they want to be seen and respected as individuals, and this is where the tiresome and time-consuming bit comes in. It is, however, the only real way you can measure your standing in the electorate. Again a sexual analogy is useful (it is surprising how often this is the case in politics, and it is best not to delve too deeply into the reasons). Most people know the story of the man who stood on a busy street corner for a day and propositioned every woman who came past; he received a lot of knock-backs and some minor personal injuries and was the subject of several police reports, but he also got laid. I am not suggesting you offer your voters sex, except perhaps as a last resort (although there is no need to look a gift horse in the mouth, as it were). But you do have to do the rounds, over and over again, and you will rarely be thanked for it, much less offered support – and in any case the promises of voters will often be as hollow and meaningless as the promises of your political colleagues.

Politicians who swear they have personally knocked on every door in their electorates are invariably liars, but you should at least attempt to make yourself known to a majority of households in areas where the votes are vital. The only real exceptions will be those residences where the garden sports a huge billboard urging a vote for your opponent. People who go to that amount of trouble can generally be assumed to have made up their minds.

Where you can't make the physical effort to ensure face-to-face contact, the wonders of modern technology and a gigantic taxpayer-funded postal allowance can help – although of course in your first, crucial grab at the seat you will have to rely on funds grudgingly supplied by the party, your friends and supporters and, horror of horrors, yourself. But at least you can make sure they are well directed. What is laughingly called 'personalised' mail is now all the rage – I say laughingly because in fact actual persons are involved only at the technical periphery. Your handwriting can be scanned and reproduced – even improved – to make it appear that you have painstakingly scrawled a note to every resident in the constituency, or at least all those with their names on the electoral roll, who are the only ones who exist as far as you are concerned.

The census breakdowns and other publicly available survey material will give you enormous amounts of information about the demographics of your electorate – how many own their own homes, their general level of income, popular sports and recreations, religion, ethnic background – in some cases the detail can come down to separate street blocks, or even to individual households. Use it ruthlessly. Think of it not as an invasion of your constituents' privacy, but as a genuine and sincere attempt to ascertain their needs and aspirations so that you can help them, or at least promise to do so every three years or so. Check up on their children and where they go to school – not as something to be used as a threat (although I suppose this could always be a last resort) but as the basis of yet another promise.

Be especially on the lookout for what might be called the

captive groups: caravan parks, hospitals and nursing homes. It is much harder for the residents to escape your attention if they are confined in advance. Many an otherwise undistinguished politician has outlasted more brilliant rivals simply by cultivating – indeed, nailing down – the votes of the aged and infirm. And of course, if you can get the matron on side, so much the better. Desperate candidates have been known to persuade a friendly matron acting as unofficial returning officer to reject the ballots of those who wish to vote for an opponent on the grounds that the patients attempting to cast them were quite clearly *non compos mentis* at the time. An even more devastating strategy used to apply in outback regions where acquiescent officials were sent to 'assist' tribal Aborigines with their votes: 'So, you like this Labor man, do you? You want him for your member? All right, you give him four votes, see, you put number 4 beside his name. You give next fella three votes, then two for this man. And this man, Country-Liberal Party man, you really hate him? Then you give him just one vote, put number 1 beside him ...' A little harmless misdirection assures the correct result; this is what is known in less fortunate countries as 'guided democracy'.

And in this context, always remember that there is a huge difference between your role as a local member and your position within your party of choice. When talking to disgruntled voters, do not hesitate to bag the government, even if you are technically of the same persuasion. Emphasise that your loyalties are first and foremost to your constituents, the people who have given you the signal honour of representing them. Lay it on with a trowel; voters, the upstart swine, have an overweening sense of their own importance, and it costs nothing to pander to it. Indeed, it is perfectly permissible to effectively disown your party and even your leader in the course of an election campaign; if claiming to be a virtual independent is the only way you can hold the seat, then go for it. In the aftermath you will seldom be blamed: both leader and party will be so grateful that you have given them another number with which to secure government that they are more likely to reward than censure you.

Things have changed; while a large majority of voters used to give their allegiance to a party rather than an individual (and many still do; it is safe to assume that at least half the votes in any seat are rusted on one way or the other, although it remains difficult to discover which half) there is an increasing trend to regard loyalty to a party, especially to one of the major parties, more as a negative than a positive. For this reason it is sensible to be a bit wary about inviting party big wigs such as ministers or shadow ministers to take a major part in your campaign. Not only are they likely to overshadow you, which is not what you want while you are struggling to get the voters to recognise your name; they may be people to whom at least a few swinging voters in the electorate have taken a personal dislike, and as a result these voters will reject you through guilt by association.

Such visits by VIPs are really more for the party faithful than for the all-important swingers; they renew the zeal of those anonymous but essential servants whose duty it is to man polling booths and stuff envelopes. As such they are pretty much a necessity of political life, but it is often best to hold them well away from election time when your loyal supporters can enjoy them and the rest of the electorate is unlikely to notice. The VIPs involved will probably thank you; during campaigns they are usually flat out with their own concerns (and in many cases reintroducing themselves to their own electorates, which they have tended to take for granted while savouring the delights of high office).

There will be times, of course, when the faceless planners, spinners, pollsters and astrologers at head office deem your base the ideal launching pad for a major rally, speech or just photo opportunity for the glorious leader; since there is nothing you can do about this, lie back and enjoy it and at least try to get in on the edge of the picture. And please, please liaise with the leader's staff. These days he is unlikely to get your name wrong – although it is still known to happen. But he might very easily be embarrassingly confused about the electorate itself. In 1972 Billy McMahon waxed long and lyrical about the quality of the sheep he had passed while driving through the marginal seat of Eden-Monaro; his farm-based audience shuffled uncomfortably at the revelation that the former minister for primary industry was still unable to distinguish sheep from the dairy cattle that are the sole inhabitants of the region's pastures. On another level New South Wales Premier Bob Carr once spoke at Byron Bay of his government's unparalleled record in creating national parks in northern New South Wales. The speech would have resonated more with his greenie audience if his transport minister, Carl Scully, had not at that very moment been driving a motorway through the shire's most loved nature reserve.

You yourself, of course, will never make such an unforced error, having diligently studied the history, geography, geology, botany, zoology, entomology, palaeontology, philosophy, psychology, criminology and above all psephology of your beloved electorate – or at least having a devoted staff member who has. The latter is surprisingly easy to find; among those who do not see themselves as front-liners there are still a large number of hard-working, idealistic individuals who are willing and able to serve without any recognition except the satisfaction of seeing their candidate (you!) advancing steadily towards his goal. Use them, indeed exploit them, by all means; but do not, repeat not, have sex with them – and I don't mean just in the literal Bill Clinton sense: don't get involved with them at all.

I know, I know; Ben Chifley did, Jack McEwen did, and innumerable others did, do and will. But it is generally a mistake. To your staff you should remain unattainable – the good family man you present to the rest of the electorate. This of course does not mean you need to be celibate or even chaste; Parliament House, as you will find when you get to Canberra, offers a voluptuous smorgasbord for your delectation. But keep it out of the office, or at least don't shit in your own nest. And while I'm at it, expand the idea of your nest to include the whole of the electorate. There is a deep contradiction in the idea of trying to become known to every man, woman and child in your constituency while at the same time trying to carry on clandestine affairs with a select few of them. Eventually you want the place to become known as 'Bentley territory', in the same way as Al Grassby once tried to redefine the Riverina as 'Grassby country' (it was in fact far better known as the headquarters of Robert Trimboli's marijuana mafia, but let that pass). You do not, however, want it identified with Bentley paternity suits.

Which brings me to the last point: distasteful as it may appear, you will have to buy property in the electorate and reside in it – for a time at least. The voters have not yet accepted globalisation to the extent that they will tolerate their representative setting up headquarters in the Bahamas or the French Riviera. But be assured that this need only be temporary. As long as you maintain an address in the electorate, after a few years you can move discreetly to a more salubrious neighbourhood on the strength of your well-earned parliamentary salary and perquisites and the credit lines that will inevitably be extended to you. Indeed, it would be wise to have several places of residence. Many politicians do. You never know when you might need them.

Best wishes from your ever-hopeful uncle,
Mungo.

SEVEN

In which we study the black art of campaigning for fun and profit

My Dear Jack,

I note with interest your plans for your election campaign and of course wish you all the best; but with all the goodwill in the world, I feel they may be just a touch extravagant. I have no desire to be a wet blanket, but perhaps you should reconsider your idea for a gala opening in which you ride down the main street on a highly decorated circus elephant while the local high school band attempts the grand march from *Aida*. You are correct in assuming that such an event would attract attention – from the police, among others; but it really seems a little flamboyant for the first-timer.

Generations of young politicians have found the trusty VW Kombi van with a simple message inscribed on the side more than adequate to the task, provided, of course, that the bloody thing doesn't keep breaking down, a contretemps which can lead to much sneering. A megaphone can be hired for a small amount and the simple message that Jack Bentley is the man for whatever the name of your electorate is regurgitated until it becomes part of the local patois.

Do not be too alarmed if the crowds do not gather immediately; the aim is to have the message sink into their subconscious until, eventually, they will come to vote for you by reflex. If you have something more specific to add, like the time and place of one of your meetings, a burst of martial music will often attract listeners. If all else fails, a verse or two of *Greensleeves* will bring the children, and with any luck at least some of their parents will follow.

We have already noted the suitability of your new name where slogans are concerned, but again caution is indicated. Your suggestion of 'Jack Bentley will take you for a ride' is at best equivocal. It is always safest to keep it simple. How about 'Jack Bentley – powerful and safe'? And for future elections, just 'Bentley – tried, tested and true'. Or perhaps not; some smartarse is bound to turn it to 'tried and convicted'. Still, the possibilities are myriad.

You are also keen on the idea of a campaign song, but again I urge second thoughts. Many years ago in my carefree youth I ran a campaign for one Jack (see how the name keeps cropping up) Grahame, and since it was in the time of the so-called swinging sixties I involved a jazz band and wrote a song. This led to the candidate being christened 'Jingle Jack' in the electorate – not such a bad thing as it at least meant a form of recognition. However, the problem with songs is that if they are simple enough to be memorable, they are also simple enough to be easily parodied. My unaffected lyrics were swiftly transformed into unkind, even scurrilous, suggestions about Grahame's personal habits, which soon echoed around the pubs of his electorate. The exercise was, I fear, counterproductive.

This leads me to the way you should treat your opponents in the forthcoming contest. The ideal answer is with indifference, or at best disdain; do not, as the modern cliché has it, give them the oxygen of publicity by so much as mentioning their names. But unfortunately this is not always practicable. You may, for instance, need to try to tie up the preferences of at least some of the minor parties and independents. This exercise is best left to your loyal lieutenants; remain aloof from such sordid negotiations if it is at all possible. Then, when your principal opponent makes outraged allegations of sinister and corrupt bargains being struck, you can truthfully plead ignorance and, if necessary, make a scapegoat of the aforementioned loyal lieutenant.

It need hardly be said that actual money should not change hands on such occasions. However, a discreet offer to help with printing costs, postage, food, drink, women or whatever can usually be brushed aside as just part of the political process. After all, there are plenty of precedents. For many years it was an open secret that the Liberal Party fed, watered, financed and generally sustained the Democratic Labor Party, especially in Victoria, and the DLP faithfully returned the preferences that Libs needed to keep them in office. There have been rumours that from time to time Labor has performed similar services for the Greens. And among individual candidates such deals are commonplace, which means that neither party really wants to make an issue of it in case it rebounds (sexual misconduct, of course, is treated with an equally blind eye and for the same reason).

You may find that your principal opponent is also bidding for the favours of the minors and independents; indeed, of course he is if he has any sense. You may be able to convince some of those up for auction that they should stick with you just because the policies of your party are more compatible with their own than those of your opponent, but don't count on it. Victory in such cases normally goes to the highest bidder. And note that we are not talking here about elections for state upper houses, where dummy parties with attractive names are routinely set up to funnel preferences to the big boys, or where parties are invented with the express purpose of collecting preferences from other fringe players and thus ensuring their founders a comfortable sinecure for at least the next eight years. We are talking about straightforward elections for the House of Representatives, where all – well, certainly most – of the candidates can be assumed to be fair dinkum.

There may also be those with whom it is unwise to have any contact at all. The various neo-Nazi groups that periodically spring up, usually from the soil cultivated by the League of Rights, are best regarded as beyond the bargepole; except perhaps in the backblocks of Queensland contact with them is seen by the mainstream as close to selling your soul to the devil, and brings condemnation from both sides of politics. One Nation, despite attempts to reform and respectabilise it, is almost equally anathema; placing it anywhere other than at the bottom of your how-to-vote card risks losing more votes from the mainstream than you are ever likely to pick up in preferences. But the others are by and large fair game, there to be used to maximum advantage through schmoozing and bribery – though never, as I have made clear, by the direct exchange of brown paper bags outside the polling booth.

Having dealt with the *hoi polloi*, how then should you treat your real opponent? The correct answer, which may surprise you, is: with the utmost respect. I know, I know: the temptation is to go to town on his weak eyesight, poor complexion, dandruff and halitosis, to cast doubt on his intelligence, sincerity and ancestry, to deride his politics and personal habits. But don't. The electorate has made it clear that, for the moment at least, it has had enough of name-calling. This is, of course, the rankest hypocrisy on the part of the voters: they themselves are willing to believe the most outrageous lies about politics and politicians, provided that they do not come from other politicians. Thus it is perfectly sound to have your supporters spread as much defamatory gossip as they can think up, provided that it can never be sourced back to you personally.

In the course of the campaign you will probably be asked about the filthy rumours which are circulating (indeed you certainly will, even if you have to get a stooge to do it). Reply along lines like: 'Well, of course I've heard stories – I suppose everyone has – (this will make those who have not rush to the pub to check them out) – but really, I'd like to keep this campaign on a higher level than that. I want to talk about policy, not personalities.' Outrageously, you can even add: 'I leave that sort of thing to my opponents.'

John Howard has alway been a master at this sort of disclaimer, in spite of having a whole section of his inner cabal dedicated almost exclusively to spreading libel about his opponents. Not just politicians but governors-general, High Court judges, church leaders, high-ranking academics and any number of lesser lights have been comprehensively smeared by Howard's operatives. But the Leader, of course, stands aloof and knows nothing. Very occasionally this can change; it was Howard himself who introduced the idea that Kim Beazley lacked the ticker to become prime minister, a brilliantly

contrived calumny that stuck to Beazley until his resignation from the party leadership and afterwards. But in general, denigration is best left to underlings.

And although it sometimes seems that the credulity of the electorate knows no bounds when believing the worst of politicians, it helps if the libel is at least consistent. At various times Gough Whitlam was accused of being in the pay of the unions and big business, of the CIA and the KGB, of Israel and the PLO. He was credited with sexual impotence, homosexuality and satyriasis. He was said to be prone to irrational rages but utterly calculating and without emotion of any kind. It is fair to say that at some stage or other quite a lot of people believed one or more of the stories, but in the end they more or less cancelled each other out.

In your own instance the idea of accusing your opponent of being an undercover member of al-Qaeda has superficial merit, but tends to strain belief when the said opponent is in fact a third-generation Australian named James Fortescue. Your ingenious solution of claiming that he was actually christened Abdullah bin Fortescue is unlikely to convince the doubters. And anyway, it might be wiser not to raise the issue of name changes, at least for an election or two.

Now to the overall conduct of your campaign. In general it is probably best to eschew gimmicks. Attend football matches, certainly, but do not be tempted to perform a celebrity kick-off; a Labor member named John Gayler was once ignominiously carried from the field after spraining his ankle in the attempt. Baby kissing is still *de rigueur*, unfortunately, but do take care that the infant involved is of a very tender age and that no suspicion of child molesting is likely to

result. It is best not to judge pet shows, which can lead to bitter recriminations from the losers, or beauty contests, which are increasingly seen as exploiting women; even if you are not as crass as Jeff Kennett, who told the contestants that he had a prize he'd like to give out if any of them would come back-stage with him later, take care to avoid any accusation of male chauvinist piggery.

Most invitations should of course be accepted but there are some to which you will give the instant flick. Members of groups which believe that the earth has been invaded by three-headed monsters from the planet Zurg may have votes, but to associate with them is to risk an overall net loss of both support and credibility. A touch of eccentricity is fine, but you don't want to be branded a complete nutter. You can and should, however, confess to a special cause or two; lines like 'I know I may seem obsessive on the subject, but one thing I hate with an unreasoning passion is cruelty to innocent chil-dren or helpless animals' invariably go down well, and require absolutely no action on your part (if anyone actually stands you up and asks what you are doing about it, point out sor-rowfully that these are really areas that come under the state government and refer them to the local state member; this is a tactic you will use frequently once you have become elected).

By now you should have finished door-knocking, although it is still a handy excuse for avoiding unwelcome invitations – 'Look, I'm really sorry, but I'll be out door-knocking that night; I feel I should try to meet the whole of the electorate, not just special interest groups.' You should, however, remain visible in the community as much as possible. Hang around shopping malls as much as you can, but warn the store holders and police in advance so that you do not get moved on for loitering with intent. Wave to people cheerily, whether you know them or not; with any luck they will have seen your picture in the press or even on television and will be vaguely flattered by the acknowledgement. Offer help to those in wheelchairs, but not to those pushing shopping trolleys; there has been quite a bit of petty theft in supermarkets recently and you don't want any misunderstandings.

All these tactics should be reconsidered if you reach high office; there is nothing phonier or more embarrassing than a ministerial 'street walk' in which a politician and his minders, surrounded by a scrum of reporters brandishing cameras and microphones, seek out some hapless passer-by for a photo opportunity. Billy Snedden was particularly inept at this; he would grab someone from a queue at a bus stop and demand 'Waiting for a bus, are you?' or accost a woman weighed down by Woolworths bags with a cheery: 'I suppose you've been doing the shopping.' More often than not, the reply was along the lines of 'Piss off', which was sometimes censored out by sympathetic editors, but quite often not. However, in the absence of a critical media, this kind of exposure can only be beneficial to a backbencher. Always remember the three Rs: Recognition, Recognition and more Recognition.

You should have at least one public meeting. It is likely that some busybody community organisation will run a 'meet the candidates' function anyway, but this is likely to be stacked by pressure groups who will want you to be absurdly specific about what you stand for. You can hardly avoid this chore, but keep it in perspective; the main thing is to avoid saying anything that can be used against you. Most of those present will probably be political activists who have already made up their minds and there are few new votes to be won. However, you might as well make the most of it; make sure you have a couple of stooges in the audience both to throw you up a Dorothy Dix question and also to embarrass your main opponent. He will probably have done the same, so if you are asked anything too pointed, glare accusingly at your opponent and say: 'Yes, well we all know who wrote that question for you.' More often than not you'll be right, and even if you're not you will have deflected the need to answer it.

Your own meeting, of course, will be stacked with supporters; you should have a couple of largish lieutenants on hand to keep serious dissidents out. Any that get through can be put in their place with lines like: 'Listen to them, ladies and gentlemen; they're not interested in democracy or free speech. They don't want to hear the truth,' and similar put-downs. The abovementioned Billy Snedden, who always had a tendency to go over the top, once assailed a group of peaceful protesters as 'political bikies pack-raping democracy', which certainly lost him the bikie vote and probably a few others beside. There is no need to go to such extremes, but always make it clear that yours is the voice of reason while your opponents represent the very brink of anarchy.

And of course, your stooges can once again be brought into play, this time not only for patsy questions, but also for seemingly hostile interjections to which you have already prepared a devastating reply. Many a reputation has been made in this manner; indeed, more than one reputation has been made out of the same put-down. The following crusher is usually attributed to Winston Churchill:

Female interjector: If you were my husband I'd put poison in your tea.

Speaker: Madam, if you were my wife, I'd drink it.

But it has also been claimed by Australia's fourth prime minister, George Reid. It is probably best not to recycle this one again, but it is not hard to set up something a little less classic.

Interjector: Why won't you do something about crime?

Speaker: I wouldn't want to put you out of a job. No, but seriously …

A bit crude, but that's just off the top of the head. I'm sure you and your brains trust can do much better.

And of course, make sure it's reported. I assume you've been cultivating your local newspaper and radio station, working your way into them at every opportunity. This isn't as hard as it sounds, because such organisations invariably operate on a shoestring and will generally leap at the prospect of free material, however tedious. Try not to make all your contributions blatantly political; contribute to the public debates as often as possible and the reporters will start contacting you automatically when anything controversial comes up.

These days you can usually expect a decent run at election times, because most of the local outlets are now part of large networks and the editors are less likely to be pushing a party line. It was not always thus. At the start of his political career Doug Anthony took the precaution of marrying into the Budd family, which controlled both the local newspaper and the local radio station. When a commercial television station came to the area the Budds thoughtfully acquired a controlling interest in that too. It need hardly be said that Anthony got a pretty good run over the years and that his Labor opponents were seldom heard of. It is perhaps not entirely coincidental that since the major networks have absorbed the local media the Anthony family's grip on the seat of Richmond, once positively feudal, has become marginal.

The media tend to overestimate their political influence, a subject to which we shall return. But of course it is always better to have them with you than against you, especially at election time. And remember that money spent on advertising in the local media is seldom wasted. In a struggling little weekly paper a half-page ad buys a hell of a lot of editorial goodwill, and the same goes for 30 seconds on radio.

Television, of course, is best of all and time is surprisingly cheap. The problem is making an ad which looks marginally professional. Among your supporters there are bound to be a couple of amateur video types. At some stage they will probably offer to help. Throw them out of the room immediately and should they persist set the dogs on them and take out an Apprehended Violence Order. Even the most favourable media treatment will seldom win an election, but appearing on television in an amateur video will infallibly lose it.

All the best from your largely Luddite uncle,
Mungo.

EIGHT

In which Uncle Mungo describes the appropriate etiquette for functions before and after the election

My Dear Jack,

I'm glad to hear you're going to be sensible about the election campaign and stick to something pretty low key. I know it's hard to pass up suggestions like an underwater meeting in a shark tank, a group parachute jump carrying banners and fireworks, or a giant blow-up image of your opponent to be ceremonially punctured on the eve of polling day. My, you do have a creative little group around you, and would you please send me some of whatever it was you were all smoking.

But on the whole it is still best to conduct your first campaign in a more or less traditional manner. You will find that in the long run nothing can replace the hard slog. Well, actually, that's a lie: huge amounts of money can, and in that context I congratulate you on securing the sponsorship of the local pet food supplier. But even the inclusion of your photo with every Newfoundland-sized pack of Doggie Dins is unlikely to obviate the need for a fair bit of old-fashioned groundwork.

You will, I fear, have to do a bit of fundraising yourself; prepared for a stupefying round of trivia nights, cake stalls and barbecues at which you will be required to purchase endless raffle tickets and lucky door tokens, not to mention several

lifetimes' supply of homemade plum jam. You will also be expected to consume at least your own weight in burned sausages and warm beer, but in regard to the latter some caution is indicated.

I have written elsewhere about the perpetual floating ALP barbecue which wends its way from location to location, pausing only to replenish supplies but somehow always forgetting the ice. The Libs have their own equivalent, and I recall with pleasure Billy Snedden doing the thank-you speech at one such event in Queensland in the early '70s. Snedden had perhaps overindulged slightly in the XXXX, and proceeded thus: 'Well, first I'd like to thank the good ladies of the branch for providing such a scrumptious repast, and old Jack here for fixing up the hall, and Fred for getting us the sound system and his lovely wife for the flowers, and well, I'm sure there are other people I've forgotten, but who gives a fuck.' Not all the plum jam north of the Tweed could compensate.

The only thing to do at such functions is to lie back and think of Canberra, and if you can get hold of any of those pills that are supposed to galvanise your bladder for the duration, that's not a bad idea either. And do keep a record of what you have spent, both for your own tax purposes and for any stickybeaks from the Electoral Commission who might take an unhealthy interest in your affairs in times to come. It doesn't have to be an accurate record of course, although it is best to avoid claiming to have been at two different fundraisers at the same time. The mere production of anything resembling a diary or an account book will send investigators into paroxysms of delight, because they can then inform their own superiors that all is well. It is only decent to look after them.

And so, at last, the sun rises on election day, as, traditionally, do many of the dead, but this is not something for the clean-cut young candidate to dwell on. It hardly needs to be said that you and your chief of staff have already prepared a battle plan (this use of military terminology, incidentally, is quite deliberate. Your shitkickers who stuff envelopes and man polling booths will have their self-esteem and enthusiasm mightily enhanced if they see themselves as heroic volunteers in the ANZAC tradition rather than the ill-treated slaves they really are).

Your sincerely smiling face, firm but fair, has already been plastered over every legal site in the district and many which are not. Banners have been prepared and large young men deputed to place them at the absolute minimum legal distance from the booths, with instructions to explain to rivals that their own attempts to pre-empt the space are against the law and that it would be in the best interests of their health insurance no-claim bonuses to remove them forthwith. Forests have been felled to provide your how-to-vote cards and a minimum of three people rostered on to each booth for every hour of voting time (one to guard each of the approaches and a spare to fill in at toilet breaks). And of course, you will have covered pre-poll and absentee votes as far as humanly possible by offering to do everything short of actually filling in the ballot papers to help those who may not be around on the day itself to do the right thing.

But with just 24 hours to go, one last ambush remains: the last-minute scare. Here, timing is all. You have to get in while there are still enough hours left to make sure your warnings are read, but not enough for your opponent to learn of the tactic and denounce it as an outrageous lie. Around Friday lunch hour is generally considered the best moment to strike. A copybook example came in 2001 when Larry Anthony, a junior minister in the Howard government, was struggling in the family's dynastic seat of Richmond. A particular area of concern was the large number of caravan parks in the electorate, whose residents felt they had been dudded by the application of the GST to their site rentals and were threatening retribution.

Then, just as they were preparing to go to the polls and wreak it, leaflets were tucked under every van door revealing that Labor had a secret plan to remove the dreaded asylum seekers from the detention centres and relocate them in (you guessed it) caravan parks. It was too late for Labor's comprehensive denial to be heard; Anthony retained his seat, but (of course) knew absolutely nothing about this devastating act of electoral terrorism, and nor did anyone else.

Such masterstrokes are best improvised at the eleventh hour; it is hard to plan them in advance as circumstances can change. But it can be noted that the most effective generally involve some appeal to the innate racism and xenophobia of the Australian electorate. And of course, once again the Goebbels principle comes into play: the more absurd the accusation, the more likely it is to be believed, at least in the heat of the moment.

On the day itself there is nothing much you can do except put in a confident appearance at as many booths as possible (but don't try to vote at more than one of them; you should be too well known by now to get away with it. Some of your anonymous supporters, however … but no, incitement to break the law is itself a crime. It is, however, a fact that there are no serious checks of identity at the booths and post-polling checks invariably reveal numerous incidents of multiple voting – although, the Electoral Commission insists, never enough to affect the result. Still, there's always a first time).

You will have to host a party for your loyal supporters after the polls close, and you should be reasonably generous – party pies as well as sausage rolls, and cask wine for the women as well as beer for the blokes. After all, win or lose, you're going to need them again, and you should try to leave them feeling wanted and appreciated.

And then it's just a matter of waiting. Do not be too eager to claim victory or concede defeat; if anyone's going to go off prematurely and look like an absolute goose, it'd be far better that it should be your opponent. Different things happen at different booths and preferences do not always behave as you might expect. The most notorious example of the unwisdom of jumping the gun came in 1961 in the Queensland electorate of Moreton, where the sitting Liberal, Jim Killen, looked gone for all money when counting stopped on Saturday night. The Communist Party candidate had collected a swag of votes, and it seemed obvious that his preferences would go to Labor ahead of Killen.

What the excitable overlooked was that the Communist was at the top of the ballot paper with Killen above his Labor opponent; the votes were not actually intended for the Communist, but were a manifestation of the so-called donkey vote, in which the ignorant and the confused (then as now a depressingly large percentage of the electorate) vote straight down the paper. The Communist's preferences thus flowed to Killen, and his seat delivered the cliff-hanger election to Menzies and the coalition. Labor's Arthur Calwell never really recovered from the defeat and Killen himself, snubbed by Menzies, invented a story that his leader had congratulated him in the words: 'Killen, you are magnificent.' Perhaps as a result of his deception, Killen was regularly passed over for the ministry until Menzies retired.

There are all sorts of morals to be drawn from this miniseries, but the most obvious is that it ain't over till the returning officer says it's over – and even then there's always the Court of Disputed Returns. But this really is the last resort; it almost never overturns a poll that has already been declared, and to appeal to it and be knocked back can earn you the lifelong reputation of a bad sport and a sore loser. It is always best to accept defeat gracefully: a manly handshake, a clap on the back and the jovial warning: 'Now, you look after my people, won't you? Because I'll be keeping an eye on you – and, of course, on your wife and kids during your frequent absences in Canberra.' This last, *sotto voce*, can begin the job of destabilising your opponent while the ink is still drying on the declaration. As always, there's not a moment to lose.

And, as you are gracious in defeat, be humble in victory. No matter how elated you feel, do not leap in the air screaming, 'We beat the bastards!' or make nose-thumbing and ear-wiggling gestures at your opponent and his supporters. When you return to what has now become your victory party, do not regale your own supporters with a few rousing variations on that old favourite, 'The working class can kiss my

arse, I've got a bludger's job at last.' Keep your gloating for the privacy of your own home. It will be no less sweet for being yours and yours alone. And of course, if you lose, you can always take it out on the wife or the dog.

But let us assume that, somehow, you've won – if not on the first time around, then on the second, third, seventh – it doesn't really matter. Before you jump aboard that great silver bird for Canberra, make sure you have secured your home base. It is precisely at this moment of triumph that your trusted electorate assistant should whisper in your ear: 'Remember you are only a member for the next three years or less, depending on the whim of the prime minister.' This may be a touch wordier than the traditional *memento mori* offered to celebrating Roman generals, but the message is the same: all glory is transitory – unless, of course, you take the appropriate measures to hang on to it and shaft any bastard who tries to take it away from you.

This means, above all, looking after the electorate. For this you will need a loyal and selfless caretaker to keep the voters happy while you are enjoying the fleshpots of Canberra, and of course the taxpayer will pick up the tab. Be smart: find someone who is neither a blood relative nor a close friend, and above all do not see this as the first of many opportunities to repay favours. There will be plenty of chances for nepotism and patronage in the years to come, and this post is simply too vital to be treated as a job for the boys (or girls). What you need is a devoted retainer who is content to live her (it is more likely to be a her) life out through your career; someone who might yearn for a fuller relationship (which of course you would never even consider) but will settle for existence by proxy, who will be satisfied simply to share your own struggles and victories on a second-hand basis; one content to serve by standing and waiting, as the poet has it.

Perhaps surprisingly, such people are relatively easy to find, especially in these troubled times; there are so many unfortunates who feel they have left behind any hope of controlling their own lives that you are likely to be killed in the rush when you advertise for a helper who will be touched, however indirectly, by the power and glamour of federal politics. Henry Kissinger described power as the ultimate aphrodisiac, which, as you will find in your subsequent adventures, is pretty accurate. But it has an attraction beyond the merely sexual; it fulfils some atavistic longing in its own right. The fact that your devoted assistant will spend most of her waking hours answering requests for assistance, many of them loony and not a few abusive, from those even more alienated and frustrated than herself matters not at all. A frisson of masochism is part of the attraction. And she will feel amply repaid by your tales of the smoke-filled rooms in which you rub shoulders with the great and powerful and the moments of high drama as you hold your peers electrified by your oratory in the house, some of which may even be true as time goes on. Of course, the fortnightly cheque from the Commonwealth of Australia helps too.

And so to Canberra. This is the turning point in your working life; you may well have already used up half of it in reaching this watershed. You are still a long way from real power – and if you haven't already realised this, you will be severely shocked when you take your place as a humble backbencher. But you have made a start, and it is time to embrace

111

a new *modus operandi*, a new credo. For the next few years at least, adopt this as your primary article of faith, the one unchanging verity in your life:

The worst thing that can happen to the country is for you to lose your own seat.

Your political survival is no longer just a matter of self-interest; it has become one of patriotism, a concern for the well-being of your fellow Australians.

To combine this with your original motivation – the unbridled lust for power – will take an element of what that unparalleled observer of politics, George Orwell, described in his novel *1984* as doublethink: the ability to hold two apparently contradictory beliefs at the same time. This may sound like a symptom of insanity, but with most truly successful politicians it becomes second nature. It is precisely because of your massive ambition, your overweening self-confidence, your absolute certainty that you know what is right for the nation and its citizens, that you are so vital to the body politic; conversely, it is the knowledge of your indispensability that gives you the will and assurance to press ahead. Now is the time to cast out self-doubt, humility, sense of proportion and above all any feeling for the absurd. These are the weaknesses that will, in time, make you a loser. The history of Australian politics is strewn with the corpses of those who failed to take themselves seriously enough.

A particularly tragic example was the most likely prime minister never to make it, Andrew Sharp Peacock. Almost from birth he was groomed for the top job: the right parents, the right education, the right social upbringing. He inherited the blue-ribbon seat of the great Sir Robert Menzies as the youngest member of the parliament of his day; he had a radio voice, television looks and an easily seductive style. He never had to worry about preselection wrangles or any other threats to his continued election; his chums in the Melbourne Club slapped down any hint of opposition to their protégé. He progressed easily through the ministry, handled a broken marriage with aplomb, took only the most presentable of mistresses and became an admired and envied member of the politico-diplomatic jet set during his days as foreign minister. To show strength and independence he even made a brief show of rebellion against his prime minister, Malcolm Fraser. When Fraser resigned after losing the 1983 election, Peacock waltzed into the leadership.

Since federation, the conservatives had never been in opposition for more than two terms; it seemed only a matter of time before the political cycle delivered the top job on a plate. But there was one last hurdle; as his far more ruthless and determined rival John Howard detected early in Peacock's term as leader, the man lacked the ultimate killer instinct. He had self-belief – with his background he could hardly have avoided it – but not absolute trust in his own supremacy. Worse, he could see the silly side of politics; it was basically a game – a very important game, certainly, but not the be-all and end-all of life. He did not believe, as the humourless Kissinger did, that his decisions had the power to change the world, for better or for worse. And he did not believe that the world would end if he lost an election.

Which, of course, he did; two of them, in fact, and the second, in 1990, he was definitely expected to win. After that debacle he was asked if he still wanted to be prime minister,

and replied, with devastating honesty: 'I'm not sure that I ever did.'

It was a terrible moment for politicians of all persuasions, and should only be remembered as a frightful warning to those temperamentally unsuited to the job to get the hell out of it. You, I am sure, have no such qualms. You are as positive about your infallibility as any pope. But, as more than one pope has found, that doesn't mean you don't have to watch your back. No matter how glorious the martyrdom, at the end of the day – at the end of eternity, for that matter – martyrs are still losers.

So, onward, ever onward and upward to your new role in Canberra, with the usual encouragement from your eager uncle,

Mungo.

NINE

In which Jack is introduced to the fantastic world of Canberra and some of its inhabitants

My Dear Jack,

So you have made it. Jack Wentworth Bentley, MP – even better, MHR, because that's the chamber where the action is.

I know your thoughts as you land at Fairbairn airport in the Canberra summer, the lake sparkling in its setting of imposing buildings, with the great patches of ordered parkland exhibiting civic order and the further-off pastures symbolising agricultural wealth. As your heart beats with patriotic pride, only one question crosses your mind: How soon can I rape it?

The answer, I fear, is not very; while your election undoubtedly marks the most significant step so far in your career, you are still a long way from real power, the sort of power that makes and unmakes ambassadors, causes powerful businessmen to tremble in your presence, and forces even media superstars to take the odd, desultory bit of notice. To reach that giddy height requires a new type of dedication, an advanced technique in the politics of terror and servility.

The road to the top now leads through your colleagues rather than the mere public. While it helps to keep the punters on side, and is of course essential for your continued re-election, the public never appointed an Australian prime minister; if it did, we would have ended up with a combination of Dick Smith and Cathy Freeman. Even if the public's choice had been restricted to politicians we could conceivably, in moments of mass hysteria, have been stuck with Joh Bjelke-Petersen or Bronwyn Bishop.

Fortunately our all-wise, all-seeing founding fathers (who by no coincidence at all were all politicians themselves, with the usual healthy quota of ambition and knavery) kept the ultimate power of patronage within the political parties; they and they alone choose their leaders, and while they may occasionally pander to populism in their desire to make sure of an election victory, they are usually pretty hard headed about it — that is, the members seek maximum personal advantage.

When the ALP swapped Bill Hayden for Bob Hawke in the last moments before Malcolm Fraser called the 1983 election, Hawke's huge popularity with the general public was certainly a factor. But at least equally important was the build-up inside the party since his previous narrow defeat. Hawke's loyal canvassers spent months wooing the undecided with promises of everything from ministries to diplomatic postings in exchange for that vital vote; even those already guaranteed a portfolio were persuaded that priority would be given to their pet projects as soon as the Hawke government took power.

In the end the tide was so overwhelming that Hayden resigned rather than contest a vote he was bound to lose; but even he did not go unrewarded. In return for making a quiet exit he received the job of his choice — foreign minister — in which he indulged himself shamelessly before requesting, and receiving, the juiciest plum of all: the governor-generalship, which he used to fill in the few remaining gaps in his luxuriant itinerary before moving on to a well-funded retirement. Had all this not been in prospect it is unlikely that Hayden would have acquiesced quite so gracefully in what was, after all, a huge political humiliation.

Eventually you are going to have to persuade your colleagues to vote you into the leadership. Obviously it helps if you have at least a modicum of talent for the job (although there are desperate times when even this is regarded as superfluous; remember Billy McMahon, or more recently Alexander Downer). But be certain that few if any of your colleagues will vote for you simply because they believe you are the best hope for the party, let alone for the country as a whole. They will first want an answer to the hard question: what's in it for me? So be prepared to distribute favours, but do not be too blatant about it.

Avoid the fate of the new Liberal member who arrived full of zeal and enthusiasm, but found himself largely frozen out by the older hands. He put his name on the whip's list to speak on every possible parliamentary debate, but after several weeks had still not received the nod. One evening he was bewailing his fate in the members' bar when Jim Killen, never one to miss an opportunity, came up with a bit of advice. There was a simple solution, Killen confided. Next time, send the whip a personal note and stick a tenner in the middle of it. This was what those in the know did, and it was why they got so many guernseys in debates. Our hero was dismayed that such venality was part of the system, but agreed to try it; next day the Liberal whip, an unbending Christian named Max Fox, received his first-ever inducement. The name of the sucker who offered it is now mercifully forgotten, as was his career from that point on.

If direct bribery is your preferred method of operation, I can only suggest that you stick to state, or better still local, politics. It may be sensible to clear this matter up before we go any further. Federal government in Australia is almost entirely free of direct monetary corruption. In state administrations shenanigans involving brown paper bags are not unknown; at local council levels they are all but endemic. But in the rarefied atmosphere of Canberra money seldom, if ever, changes hands.

It would be nice to think that this is because federal politicians are, by their very nature, sea-green incorruptibles. Certainly they usually set out with loftier aims than those on the lower tiers of government and they are often smarter. But the hard fact is that the opportunities for getting on the take at the national level are very limited. It is true that the contracts involved are huge, especially in areas like defence, but there are comparatively few of them and they are subject to very close scrutiny. The everyday transactions in which palms are greased like development approvals and trading licences are not likely to involve anyone on the commonwealth level.

The single exception is Immigration, where the minister has enormous power to grant personal favours; but it must be said that no minister has ever been caught abusing that power – at least in return for money. A single member of parliament, Andrew Theophanous, has been gaoled for accepting bribes in return for attempting to use his influence in the area, but he was never part of the executive government.

I trust this has not dashed your hopes unduly; and let me

hasten to assure you that there are plenty of perfectly legal ways of making a bit of extra cash during your time in parliament, and I am sure you will have noticed that not many politicians retire broke. But for now, back to the matter at hand: your induction into Canberra, and in particular into Parliament House.

Many years ago, when parliament was still housed in the unhygienic but user-friendly premises further down the hill, Labor's wily veteran Pat Kenneally noticed a newcomer gazing around King's Hall in some bewilderment. Although the new member was not of his own political persuasion, Kenneally took pity on him and decided to offer him a little wise advice. 'Son,' said Kenneally, draping a paternal arm over the short, stout man's shoulders, 'look over there. There are two doors leading out of this hall. The one in the middle goes to the library. The one on the right goes to the bar. Be careful which one you choose; your whole career in this place depends on it.' 'Gee, thanks,' gasped Senator Vince Gair, and disappeared through the door on the right with a zeal that nearly tore it from its hinges.

But in all fairness it must be said that Gair also made good use of the library. He could frequently be found after lunch in one of its comfortable leather chairs, eyes closed in contemplation, breathing slow but regular.

If you are tempted to regard this as a cautionary tale, remember that Gair spent many happy years in Canberra as leader of the DLP, wheeling and dealing with both governments and oppositions, before being bribed (yes, the word is appropriate) out of politics with the offer of the ambassadorship to Dublin in one of the Whitlam government's more spectacular stuff-ups. Many politicians have done quite well at the bar, although taking up permanent residence there is generally considered unnecessarily brutish. Remember the great philosophers: moderation in all things, and plenty of it.

Certainly you don't want to be standoffish; the atmosphere of Parliament House lends itself to certain clubbishness, if not something more adolescent. One of the more perceptive politicians of my era, Senator John Button, once told me that with its emphasis on teams and gangs, its overwhelming maleness and its series of outdated and pointless rules, the place reminded him of boarding school. Being in one of my grumpier moods, I snapped back: 'You must have gone to a shithouse boarding school.' Button took that on board, and thereafter referred to his 'shithouse boarding school' analogy. Times have changed: the residence has been upgraded and a lot more women have been admitted. But the basic proposition still has some validity. Parliament remains a largely closed society with a very exclusive membership, which lives by its own rules. There are other inhabitants, but they are there, by and large, simply to serve the membership.

The important exception is the press gallery, which believes that the membership is there to serve it. We will deal with this awful institution at more length later, but from the very beginning be aware that you can expect no favours, nor fairness, nor even common courtesy from today's media. You have achieved public office, and are therefore fair game. This does not mean that the media cannot be used; as a class, they are almost ridiculously open to flattery, and are always desperate for a story; deals can be and regularly are done which involve trading stories for favourable mentions. But do not

think they can be bought, or even rented on any more than a very short lease. As with your colleagues, they are poised for the slightest hint of blood and decay, and will home in on it like piranhas, like jackals, like vultures, which is how they are described by most politicians and more bitterly still by the families of politicians.

Fortunately even the most disgusting scavengers have their uses. An old and oft-repeated rhyme is still apposite:

You cannot hope to bribe or twist

The fearless British journalist;

But seeing what the man will do

Unbribed, there is no reason to.

So think of the press gallery not just as a potential enemy (which, to a greater or lesser extent, is true of every single person in Parliament House and a hell of a lot of those outside it). Think of it as a potential resource. But treat it with respect; all its members have been there longer than you have on the day you arrive and some of them have been there forever; as I write this there are still men in that building who were insulted face to face by Billy Hughes. They are very conscious of their seniority; it is wise to acknowledge it.

Do not blunder cheerfully into their offices, hand outstretched, expecting to be welcomed as an equal. A young Liberal once did just that to the dreaded Ian Fitchett; bursting into the *Sydney Morning Herald* office in the early afternoon, he found the great man dozing in his chair, a handkerchief over his face. Undaunted, the eager Liberal greeted him: 'Hello, I'm Jim Forbes.' From beneath the handkerchief came the reply: 'Fuck off, Forbes.' In retrospect he got off lightly. Stories of Fitchett's put-downs are part of the gallery's history.

On one occasion while dining in a superior Melbourne hotel he signed the bill, only to be confronted by an embarrassed Italian waiter. 'Please, Mr Fitchett,' he quavered. 'Here you have written room 303. But your room, it is 309.' Fitchett eyed him with distaste. 'Why, so it is,' he grunted, making the correction. 'I must have been thinking of the gun we shot you bastards with during the war.' Even Menzies did not escape unscathed. Annoyed with something Fitchett had written about him, he pulled the reporter up in King's Hall. 'You'll eat crow for this, Fitchett,' the great man thundered. Fitchett was unabashed. 'And eat it I will sir,' he replied, 'provided it is seasoned with the sauce of your embarrassment.'

Perhaps fortunately there are no Fitchetts left; but be assured, if Laurie Oakes can ask the chief of the armed forces if he feels like a dill, he can certainly make a dill out of a neophyte member like yourself. So: introduce yourself, humbly, to the media, seeking out particularly those whose products can be read, heard and seen in your own electorate – they are the ones that matter most, but try to make yourself generally known to all, and avoid making enemies, even if they appear to have no outlet within a thousand kilometres of any of your voters. The gallery is a club within a club, a pack in its own right, and to offend one can frequently be seen as a slur on all. For the time being that is all that is necessary; when you have settled in we can discuss further the black arts involved in the peddling of influence.

You will have been allocated both an office and a seat in the house. Your seat is over on the outskirts, in an area where the television cameras never cast a glance? Tough. The prime spots directly behind the dispatch boxes on each side of the table, the ones that come into view every time the prime minister or the leader of the opposition gets to his feet, have already gone to those in the know. Similarly, there is no point in complaining about your office; indeed, you should be immensely grateful that you were not condemned to share a draughty broom cupboard with another backbencher and both your staffs, at least one of whom could be guaranteed to have halitosis and the other to fart like a horse. Such was the fate of newcomers in the old Parliament House, a venue that, for all its charm, would have been unhesitatingly condemned by the RSPCA if anyone had attempted to use it as a feedlot.

At least you now have something pretty much like a self-contained flat, however inconvenient the location. But don't be tempted to use it as such. Not only will this draw well-merited accusations of standoffishness and meanness from your colleagues; it will also mean that you Get Out Of Touch, one of the great pitfalls of a political career. No matter how diligently you use the fax machine and your email, they will not and cannot replace face-to-face contact with the outside world – or at least with the rest of Parliament House, which for most of your waking hours amounts to the same thing. You must be seen; bestride the corridors of the building, even if you infrequently meet another living soul in the process. At the very least it will be good for your figure, often an early casualty of political life.

Note also: the paranoid public servants who were in charge of the construction of the new building made it as easy as possible for politicians to avoid all scrutiny by both public and media, not to mention friends and family and even their closest colleagues – although not the security services, the inconvenience of whose surveillance far outweighs any role they may have in the protection of members. There are obviously times when privacy – indeed, absolute inaccessibility – is useful, but under normal circumstances it is better to be as open as possible while always remaining within hurtling distance of the nearest bolthole.

Enter the place, fearlessly, by way of the front steps, even if it means a brisk detour from your car park. Eat and drink at the public café, regardless of the quality of the company and the food. Become a frequenter of the gym, pool and tennis courts. Remember what I told you about learning tennis; at Parliament House it can be a great socialiser and has the inestimable advantage of being one of the few venues at which you can fraternise with outsiders – particularly journalists – on more or less equal terms and without exciting more than the usual suspicions of conspiracy. It is, of course, most unwise to dine or drink publicly with members of the press unless you want to attract attention to some special relationship. You will inevitably be blamed for any future leaks from your dining companions, even when such stories are manifestly not to your advantage.

The more you are seen around Parliament House itself, and its immediate environs, the better; and of course there are certain recognised bars and restaurants around town which are forced to accept politicians under the Non Discrimination Act, and at which at least occasional appearances are advisable. But beware of venturing too far outside the conventional boundaries; here be dragons. Under no circumstances accept social invitations unless you know exactly what you are getting yourself into. More than one eager member has taken up a casual invitation to an intimate drink, only to find himself centre stage at a meeting of wild-eyed viragos dedicated to the cause of lesbian separatism, not a good look when the pictures appear in the local paper of his suburban middle-class electorate. The other extreme can be even more daunting: a quiet rendezvous in a bar, which culminates in tabletop dancers and an invitation to judge the perfumed beaver competition. If such is your fetish, you will almost certainly find those who will cater to it, discreetly of course, within the walls of your new home.

And think of it as home. For your next few years it will be where charity begins and the heart resides, and there will be no place like it. And it should always be thought of as something you could enjoy renovating, at least as far as the personnel is concerned. In your own mind at least, start drawing up plans to redecorate the prime minister's suite and the cabinet room. There is no time to lose.

All the best from your increasingly excited uncle,
Mungo.

TEN

*In which we are warned of the joys
of the junket and the perils of the party room*

My Dear Jack,

Now that the initial shock of Canberra has worn off, it's time to start getting you seriously orientated. By that I don't mean studying a street map of the Nat Cap in order to untangle the concentric circles of spaghetti that seem to make up the road system; this is a secret reserved for the innermost councils of the National Capital Development Commission, made the more puzzling by the fact that some of them have been installed backwards, having been imported unchanged from Los Angeles where the traffic drives on the right rather than the left — a fact apparently unobserved by the eagle-eyed bureaucrats of Canberra. In future you will be conveyed through the maze by commonwealth car drivers whose job it is to get you swiftly but discreetly to your destination. Since this will seldom be other than Parliament House or the restaurants and bars generally frequented by politicians, the task is not an onerous one.

You will, however, need somewhere to stay. Consider your options carefully — much may depend on them. In the old days most members checked in either at the Hotel Kurrajong or at the Hotel Canberra, mainly because there was virtually no alternative. Some, for reasons of economy or modesty, stayed there even after things improved; as prime minister Ben Chifley famously eschewed the Lodge and remained at the Kurrajong Hotel – although cynics have suggested that this may also have had something to do with his domestic arrangements, for which see below.

As Canberra grew, some smarties took advantage of low land prices and grotesquely subsidised interest rates considered necessary to lure the inhabitants – particularly the public servants – from Sydney and Melbourne and bought their own residences, later to be sold at equally grotesque profits; this perk is still available, although, alas, the subsidies have been removed and the expectation of vast capital gains consequently reduced. Others rent, often on a share basis; with travelling allowances set at hotel rates, this can also produce a tidy profit at the end of the session.

This, of course, involves finding a like-minded co-tenant. In the late sixties ministers Leslie Bury and Jim Forbes made a wonderfully compatible double, mainly because they both liked a very large drink on a warm day; the only arguments were over whether to have whisky or brandy with their morning weeties. Another odd couple were John Howard and Warwick Parer; conspiracy theorists have since opined that Howard's unaccountably lenient treatment of Parer's blatant conflicts of interest may have indicated that Parer kept a detailed diary at the time, perhaps even accompanied by photographs.

For this reason if no other, it is probably wiser to stick by yourself, at least for the first session or two. It is best to check out the neighbours. There will be many times when you will wish to be unobserved, and if you don't, be sure that your visitors will.

Which brings us, inevitably, to the subject of sex. The first rule, of course, is to keep it out of your own office unless you are prepared for a serious long-term relationship. Such cases do exist; even such household names as Ben Chifley and John McEwen made mistresses (and in McEwen's case, eventually a wife) of their secretaries. But more often than not it ends in tears. The case of Jim Cairns and Juni Morosi, while it was at least as much about politics as lust, provides an awful example of what can happen if (as Cairns once put it) you wear your heart too easily on your sleeve — although others would claim that it wasn't just his heart that was the problem. But, as the old hands used to say, why eat at the soup kitchen when you're surrounded by five-star restaurants?

You will find that few of your colleagues observe any real form of asceticism. Some, rather ostentatiously, do; the National Party leader John Anderson extolled the virtues of chastity, so much so that he preached that those who broke the rules of marriage were too dishonest to have a place in the national parliament. All I can say is that if he had been taken seriously he would have had a pretty lonely time in the cabinet room, let alone in the parliament as a whole.

Affairs between politicians are known to take place, even across party lines. However, they are also to be discouraged, especially at ministerial level. When James Killen and Margaret Guilfoyle, both members of Malcolm Fraser's cabinet, became publicised as 'the romantic ministers', Fraser felt constrained to call them in for a reprimand — not because he was a sexual puritan, far from it, but because he felt that it was giving his government a bad image. Even at the very top, it is necessary to maintain certain standards — of hypocrisy, if

133

nothing else. At least garrulous Gareth Evans had the discretion not to brag about his affair with Cheryl Kernot.

So forget about your colleagues and personal staff; this still leaves everyone else's staff, the house staff (the library has always been a popular hunting ground for more than mere information), the press gallery, the public service, the groupies from the universities – indeed, the entire population of Canberra plus tourists and visitors. A surprising number of them will be sufficiently impressed by the magic letters MP to make further inducement unnecessary. For others – well, those allowances have to be spent on something.

The only area in which some caution is needed is that of overseas travel. Getting sprung with a mistress on a study tour in southern France can be both career and marriage threatening, as an ambitious Liberal named Bob Woods found to his cost. Nor did it help when it came out that he had told the woman involved that if there were any queries about the legitimacy of his trip, he would be able to explain it away as research into wine and cheese, and that she was acting as his adviser. There is no need for such insensate greed; you have plenty of time. A favourite gag around the place during my time involved the old bull and the young bull. The young bull says: 'Hey look, the farmer's left the gate into the cow paddock open. Let's rush down and do a couple.' The old bull says: 'No, let's walk down and do the lot.'

Travel is, of course, a sensitive issue; given the fact that the allowances involved, while adequate, are not exactly the stuff that dreams of avarice are made of, some politicians go to quite extraordinary lengths to rort them. Tony Street, a lavishly paid senior minister who also had considerable independent means, used to designate his holiday house as his principal place of residence in order to pick up a few extra bucks a week. Michael Cobb made a point of stopping his car a few metres beyond the limit at which the allowance kicked in and sleeping on the ground rather than returning home for the night. This is a lot of discomfort for a comparatively small return (of course it also gives politicians a name for being mean and tricky – sound familiar?). While there is no need for you to worry about the general image, it is best to be seen on a personal level as rising above the mire.

And of course when the rort becomes downright fraud, the wrath of the public knows no bounds. This is the sort of fiddle the voters understand only too well, and one they hate with an abiding passion because it is not available to them. They will forgive many things – lies, nepotism, the peddling of influence, the subversion of the public purse for political purposes, even the blatant misuse of privilege such as the Howard family's occupation of Kirribilli House. But if they catch you cheating on your taxi chits, they will hound you forever. It's just not worth the risk. And in fact you will find that you do quite nicely while sticking strictly within the rules – generations of your crafty predecessors have made sure that they do not suffer unduly while tirelessly serving the people.

Apart from free transport and generous living away from home allowance, you are also entitled to an overseas study tour during every term of parliament on the subject of your choice (although it's generally sensible to find something that at least sounds more serious than cheese and wine – if you really must, then at least call it Lactic and Oenological Fermentation). But these are just the normal perks of office – the everyday junkets available to everyone. Much more fun is to be had on the official parliamentary missions in which a lucky selection of backbenchers from all parties gets to represent the parliament at some generally meaningless gathering with their fellow travellers from other parliaments around the world. For the obvious reason that these functions are planned by politicians for politicians, they are invariably held in the nicer parts of the world and in conditions of considerable luxury. And because those taking part are official delegates from the Australian government, the local Australian embassy or High Commission is lined up to fill any gaps in the program the host organisation may have overlooked.

It need hardly be said that such trips are jealously sought after and that much manoeuvring is devoted to grabbing a seat in the business-class section of the plane as it leaves Australia behind and the free drinks trolley makes its first appearance in the aisle. In the true spirit of Australian democracy, the selection is usually left to a vote of the party room, and although such votes are generally subject to gentle guidance from the factional heavies and their knee-cappers on both sides of politics, it is high time we introduced you to what used to be the smoke-filled rooms where the plans were laid and the deals were done. In these enlightened days the rooms are no longer smoke-filled and most of the planning and dealing is done in the offices of the factional bosses, but the party room will still be an important venue during much of your career.

You will enter it first when the troops assemble shortly after the election is declared, in order to elect a new leader or reaffirm an old one. If your party has lost, the mood will still

VOTE 1 FOR ME YOU ANTS

be determinedly optimistic, especially if the old leader has already resigned and is no longer present; he can thus be happily blamed and blackguarded for all previous failures as soon as a formal motion has been passed thanking him extravagantly for his gallant efforts on the party's behalf. This is frequently extended to a lengthy and bitter review about what went wrong last time and what to do about it, as was the case with Labor after the 2001 disaster. Take no part in it – indeed, run for cover. Let the old guard chop each other down, while remaining clear of the carnage and ready to join the inevitable healing process when the new regime finally emerges. If, on the other hand, your party is in the process of forming government, things will be ebullient, and as a new member you will be welcomed with the kind of effusion you are unlikely to encounter again unless (until, Jack, until) you personally lead the party to victory.

If you have actually captured a seat from the other side the cheering will be even louder and if it was a seat no one expected you to win you will be, for a few moments, a veritable hero. In 1990 a totally unknown Labor candidate named Neville Newell, through an entirely fortuitous set of circumstances, won the seat of Richmond, which had been held by the National Party since federation. Moreover, he knocked off the Nationals' leader, Charles Blunt, in the process. When Newell diffidently poked his head into the party room no one had a clue who he was; someone told him brusquely to piss off, this was a private meeting. When he coyly identified himself there was a stunned silence, then a roar of acclamation; the veteran Gordon Bilney shouted, 'Run for leader!' and even Bob Hawke had the grace to laugh rather than snarl. From there on it was all downhill; Newell lasted for six years but eventually Richmond returned to the Nationals, and Newell became a footnote in federal Labor history. This, of course, is not what you want; but if you can momentarily become the centre of attention in those early days, savour it – and, unlike Newell, try to build on it. Such unequivocal applause in political life is rare indeed.

As a new member you will also be instructed in the details of what is expected from you as a backbencher, probably by the party whip. These are not difficult, and you may have heard them before: cleanliness, punctuality and unquestioning obedience to your seniors are the essentials. It will be made clear to you that your role in the decision-making processes of the party is to raise your hand when you are told to and occupy your seat in the house when it is required. Actually it isn't a bad idea to be present more often than this, especially in the first few weeks. Not only will you gain a probably undeserved reputation for diligence but you will also gain the odd insight into how the place works, who are the key figures and the mechanics of debate. And of course it will give you a chance to make yourself known – indeed, toady – to the various acting speakers and, more importantly, the clerk and his deputy. As with so many others at this early stage in your career, you never know when they may prove useful.

But back to the party room. When the house is sitting you will meet here once a week, or more in emergencies. While the main purpose of these meetings is solidarity and the inculcation of the team spirit – what is nowadays called bonding – it is not all uplifting harangues from the leader and his more articulate hangers-on. There will be times when votes are to be taken for various jobs within the parliamentary party including the aforementioned trips. These are normally occasions of great seriousness – or at least should be. On one occasion within the Labor caucus the whip was laying out the guidelines for new members. 'You must number all the candidates in order of preference from one to four,' he intoned. 'Remember. No ticks or crosses.' From the back of the room came the voice of Barry Jones: 'Only double crosses.' Such refusal to take the rituals of the party with due reverence was, of course, one of the reasons he suffered quite a few of them himself, especially during his time as ALP president.

From time to time there will be an actual debate within the party room, a debate about real policy, a debate of genuine substance. In dim and distant days these used to be almost routine, and were followed avidly by the media; questions of who said what, who insulted whom, who backed the leader and who dissented – and sometimes most intriguingly of all, who sat still and kept quiet – could be the stuff of headlines. It was common for members to leak selectively to the media, usually with a view to paying out their enemies; enhancing one's own position was considered a trifle vulgar by most.

But not by all. In the 1960s a Liberal named Les Irwin appointed himself a sort of party room correspondent for the Sydney *Daily Telegraph*. Irwin took copious notes within meetings, and immediately afterwards would go upstairs to the *Telegraph*'s office, where he dictated these to a junior reporter. His account usually included lines like: 'In a passionate and moving contribution Les Irwin, the member for Mitchell, argued convincingly and to great applause …' or 'Things were looking bad for Prime Minister McMahon until the member

for Mitchell, Les Irwin, made a shrewd and powerful inter-
vention.' Lines like these seldom appeared in next morning's
paper, but Irwin's records, however one-sided, undoubtedly
gave the *Telegraph* a useful edge. Of course everyone knew he
was doing it, but such was the grip the *Tele*'s proprietor, Sir
Frank Packer, exerted on the Liberal Party at that time that no
one dared bring the subject up, let alone try to reprimand
Irwin for his open breach of party rules. Indeed, McMahon
even nominated Irwin for a knighthood, a proposal which
was promptly vetoed by Gough Whitlam when Labor came
to power in time to rewrite the New Year's Honours List.
Whitlam later described the idea as the most extraordinary
suggestion for ennoblement since Sir Toby Belch.

These days prime ministers rarely let serious discussion
find its way into the party room; most issues are settled by the
PM and his chosen few, or at least within the confines of
the cabinet room. For this reason leaking from the party room
is no longer considered a hanging offence; most of what goes
on there is either trivial or semi-public (especially in the case
of the leader's gung-ho speechifying) already. Nonetheless,
there will be times when you can turn such things to your
advantage. The Irwin approach can be modified to suit the
circumstances of the day.

Telephoned by an eager pressman for your view of the
current state of leadership tensions within the party (and for
an eager pressman there will always be leadership tensions
within the party) you can affect reluctance: 'Of course, it's all
a bit of a beat-up as you know, but I must say I thought the
boss was a bit off his form in the party room last week. Not
anything you could put your finger on mind, but I don't know

if he's quite as keen as he was. Not that it matters, of course; he's still well and truly got the numbers, and he will have as long as he keeps his nerve. Certainly my lot – and there are probably more of us than you might think – are going to stick with him unless events move right out of control, and frankly I can't see that happening unless the other side gets its act together. That makes him safe for the moment, at least until things change.'

Entirely waffle; sheer unadulterated gobbledegook, and nothing there that can possibly get you accused of plotting or disloyalty, even if your phone was tapped and every word of the conversation taped by the leader's office. But your eager and enterprising reporter is going to have heaps of fun with it, producing yet another 'Leadership Rumblings Continue' story in which the single solid fact is that Jack Wentworth Bentley is emerging as a key player, a mover and shaker, even a king maker in the struggles that lie ahead. If this line is repeated often enough the chances are that some of your more gullible colleagues will start believing it and begin to group around you – which will make the original wholly fictional story a self-fulfilling prophecy, to the continued benefit both of the reporter involved and, far more importantly, yourself. And that, my boy, is why the party room remains important – to you, not to the party.

Regards from your anticipatory uncle,
Mungo.

ELEVEN

In which Uncle Mungo reminisces on politicians, journalists and alcohol

My Dear Jack,

You will now be growing used to your life in Parliament House, using the word 'life' in its loosest sense; it is, of course, more of a day-to-day existence – rather like conventional warfare, with periods of boredom interspersed with bursts of furious activity, the whole having an appearance of total unreality fuelled largely by adrenaline and alcohol.

Once more, a touch of Orwellian doublethink is called for: you must, of course, treat the entire business and the rituals that go with it with the utmost seriousness, but also keep at least part of yourself detached from the passions involved – a cool observer forever on the alert for a chance to exploit the weaknesses of others should they leave themselves open in an unguarded moment.

This habit is both easier and more widespread than it may appear; study the eyes of your colleagues as you attempt to engage them in conversation. They will, or at least should, appear to be paying attention, but you will find them constantly glancing elsewhere, fearful of missing the opportunity to move on to someone more important or eager to check on other seemingly random encounters: just why is that minister speaking so earnestly to that backbencher? In politics alliances are forever being made and broken. Knowledge of their current state of play is always useful.

But there will be times when you find yourself carried away by the sheer exhilaration of the process, by the excitement of being close to, though not yet in control of, the levers of power. These are the times to be careful, when the surges of alcohol and adrenaline can leave you vulnerable. It can be vital to avoid overdosing. In my last letter I touched on the need for a certain discretion in the area of sex; the same applies to the demon drink, and in no trumps redoubled.

I am not, of course, suggesting that you take up abstinence; like any eccentricity that distinguishes you from the mob, it is to be avoided at all costs. Far better to be the loud-mouthed pest who never leaves the members' bar than never to be seen in it at all. Wowsers are seldom popular – the arch example was Edward St John, whose straitlaced and censorious approach to the conduct of politics in general and John Grey Gorton in particular led first to his ostracism and later to his total humiliation. St John, his critics claimed with disgust, exuded an odour of sanctity. In vain did he insist that there were worse things to smell of; not in the members' bar there weren't. Taking the high moral ground might be a useful tactic when dealing with the mug public, but don't try it on your fellow politicians.

Not all teetotallers are wowsers; Barry Jones, for instance, was quite a jolly chap while sticking to lemon squash, and indeed achieved limited political success. But joining a drinking school is very much part of a normal day in Parliament House, and abstention on any grounds except the strictly medical is generally frowned on as appearing a bit snooty. The trick, of course, is to keep it within bounds. As the actor Dean Martin once said when asked if he drank: 'Only moderately. Come and see me after the show, I've got a case of moderately in the dressing room.'

It should be said at once that far more excessive drinkers have climbed the greasy totem pole than have abstainers. The abovementioned John Gorton comes to mind as one who reached the very top in spite of a rate of consumption which sometimes led to his failing to make it back to the Lodge and being discovered by the Parliament House cleaners next morning unconscious on a couch in the lobbies. On other mornings he would fail to turn up for work, brought down by what his long-suffering press secretary would describe as 'a touch of flu' – Gorton flu quickly became part of the language of heavy drinkers.

As did 'Forbes back' – Jim Forbes, who it will be recalled shared a flat with Les Bury in conditions of companionable insobriety, used to complain that it was his back which caused his health problems, including falling off the stage at an election rally in 1969. There were other views; once when he unwisely accused Gough Whitlam of lacking guts, Whitlam replied brutally: 'It's what he puts in his guts that's rooted him.' However, both Forbes and Bury became senior ministers in the Gorton government, although in the sweep of history that probably isn't saying very much.

Others have made a big thing of becoming reformed drunks, at least for the duration of their stay in the Lodge. But while such dramatic gestures unquestionably have a public relations value, cynics might doubt that they are strictly necessary. After all, our very first prime minister, Edmund Barton, was known to his colleagues and the public as Tosspot Toby, and it did him no harm at all either during his career or in the history books. Every government since federation has boasted at least one Olympic-class drinker; to balance up Forbes and Bury I should probably mention Lionel Murphy from Whitlam's government and Peter Walsh from that of Bob Hawke.

But there are also those who have never made it. The brash young Andrew Jones, for instance, was pilloried for asserting that half the members were half drunk half the time. If anything this was an underestimate – on Jones's figures this meant that parliament as a whole was just 12.5 per cent pissed at any given moment, or alternatively that you had the equivalent of 15 of the then 120 members of the House of Representatives totally legless, not really such a bad result by Australian standards. However, the pompous rose up in outrage and Jones was forced to recant. But like Galileo he didn't really mean it, and zealously went on to become a more or less permanent member of the 15. Eventually he was convicted of drunk driving, lost his seat and ended up in a sanatorium – perhaps not a completely different environment from his previous one, but certainly far less prestigious. Jones's fall was a spectacular one, but many others have just drifted through parliamentary life in a genial alcoholic haze, sacrificing ambition for a comfortable befuddlement. One such was Dr Dittmer, of whom you (and indeed most people) have never heard. Read on and learn from his undistinguished example.

Felix Cyril Sigismund Dittmer (what a moniker! Definitely not prime ministerial. Aren't you glad you saw my point) was a Queensland medico who, for some reason now lost in the mists of time, found himself in the senate from 1959 to 1971 – two full terms, and I do mean full. Like his fellow banana bender Vince Gair, Dittmer quickly realised that his natural habitat was the bar, with an occasional excursion to the senate chamber when he was sure the bells he heard ringing signified a division rather than a hangover. This is not to say that he neglected his duties, either parliamentary or Hippocratic. There was, for instance, the celebrated occasion when Senator Douglas Hannaford dropped dead on the floor of the chamber. His colleagues rushed him out into King's Hall where a number of the younger doctors in parliament went to work on him with mouth to mouth, heart massage and so on. Attracted by the noise, Dittmer made his way down the corridor and cast a professional glance over the frantic scene. 'No point in that,' he growled. 'Poor bugger's dead' – and returned to the bar. As it happened, Dittmer's diagnosis was spot on, although, as we shall see, matters were not always so simple.

This was the time when Whitlam was making his reputation within the Labor Party as a classy campaigner; in the late '60s he fought and won a number of by-elections, an important factor in cementing his position as leader of the party. One such contest was in the Queensland seat of Capricornia, centred on Rockhampton, which happened to be Dittmer's home base. Dittmer was therefore deputed to show his leader around the somewhat uninspiring electorate, a task he undertook with little enthusiasm. Rural elections in those days were (and to some extent still are) dreary affairs, consisting largely of sparsely attended public meetings at which a few sullen farmers complained about everything and gave no indication of how they planned to vote or even whether they would turn up. Apart from that it was a matter of nailing campaign posters to telephone poles, from which the council tore them down, or to trees, which were considered less aesthetically pleasing and therefore fair game for vandals. Whitlam insisted on varying the formula by hiring a flatbed truck from which he constantly harangued audiences of two men and a dog, with the dog usually the most attentive listener. It was a hellish week. Whitlam, being Whitlam, bore it stoically but it was enough to drive a normal man to drink. Felix Dittmer was a normal man.

So it was that one morning Whitlam found himself on the back of the truck without his local mentor. Undeterred, he began his usual spiel, only to realise after a few minutes that his audience was even more distracted than usual. Their attention was gripped by a scrabbling at the side of the truck; Dittmer, having had his sleep-in, was belatedly trying to take his place beside his leader, but was having trouble mounting the vehicle. Twice he fell back defeated. The third time he took a determined run, jumped aboard and, arms flailing, staggered past Whitlam to fall off the other side. It was undoubtedly the highlight of the campaign, and when Labor claimed victory, Dittmer rightly claimed a share of the credit.

But his interventions were not always so successful. A constant drinking companion was Senator Hartley Gordon James Cant (another of those names), of whom, like Dittmer, you have never heard. His only real claim to fame was his appearance on a party room ballot paper along with Lionel Murphy, Dorothy Tangney and Jim Poke; the paper read Murphy Cant Poke Tangney, which some insiders regarded as

a deliberate challenge. But Cant did once come to prominence in his own right when he committed the unforgivable sin of voting against his own party.

In those days the senate numbers were finely balanced, with the DLP holding the balance of power. Thus there were times when Labor and the DLP could vote together to defeat the government and score a minor political triumph; this was one of those times. Cant heard the division bells in plenty of time and staggered from the bar to his usual seat in the chamber. The problem was that this was a division in which Labor and the DLP were voting aye and the government was voting no; Cant was thus on the wrong side. He looked up to see his colleagues sitting opposite, waving and calling to him to cross over; flattered by their attention he waved back, assuring them that he was in his place, everything was fine. The bells ceased and the count was taken. The government, with Cant's help, had won, and Cant faced instant expulsion from the party.

But Dittmer determined to save his friend. Shouting that Cant was desperately ill, he ran from the chamber and called an ambulance; in the meantime the still smiling Cant was taken to his office and allowed to see no-one. Dittmer explained that he had been treating his colleague for a kidney disease and that obviously there had been a potentially fatal adverse reaction to the medication. The ambulancemen heard the end of this diagnosis and looked at each other somewhat quizzically. Nonetheless at Dittmer's insistence they loaded their patient and sped off to the emergency department at Royal Canberra Hospital. They decanted, as it were, Cant, and Felix repeated his diagnosis to the young intern in charge. The intern looked at Cant, and then looked at Dittmer.

'Are you sure you're a doctor?' he inquired. 'Oh yes,' said Dittmer, 'Felix Dittmer, MB BS Queensland University, all in order.' 'And what did you say was the trouble with this man?' the intern persisted. Dittmer put a brave face on it. 'Kidney problems,' he said firmly. 'Renal colic.' The intern looked at Dittmer and then back at Cant. 'Are you sure,' he asked, 'that you can tell the difference between renal colic and alcoholic?' In the end Cant took a week's leave of absence and the matter blew over; but Cant never entirely forgave his would-be saviour. 'You know,' he would say in later years, 'I don't really remember much about that day – those pills young Felix gave me must have really knocked me around. I was so bad I actually voted against the party. He could have done for me altogether.'

It need hardly be added that neither senator was ever considered, however remotely, to be a candidate for promotion. Yet each, in his own way, made a contribution to political life, the contribution being to stand as a warning to others.

Given the importance of the role alcohol plays in Australian political life you may find it strange that so little appears in the media. The reason is actually quite straightforward: the press gallery as a group was in those happy days even more stonkered than the party rooms, and was in no position to throw the first bottle. And many of its experiences were even more tragic.

There was the case of Eric Walsh, a drinker of Olympic standard, who at one stage contracted a sore toe. His GP diagnosed the dreaded gout, and a regimen that excluded both red wine and port. Walsh, aghast, sought a second opinion; the verdict was the same, and remained so as an increasingly desperate Walsh did the round of Canberra surgeries. But persistence was rewarded; at last, in rundown offices in a distant suburb, he located a dubious figure who assured him that in spite of all scientific evidence to the contrary, a few bottles of decent shiraz was just what the doctor ordered, and that would be thirty dollars. The gout continued, but Walsh's faith in the medical profession had been vindicated.

A less happy tale is of Richard L'Estrange, inevitably known as Dick the Odd. L'Estrange first came to prominence while accompanying Whitlam on a trip to Mexico, during which he was reluctantly dragged from the poolside bar to make a visit to the pyramids of Tenochtitlan. There he stood thirstily in the sun while a guide explained how on the summer solstice a priest of the sun would sacrifice a virgin by tearing out her heart in front of a frenzied crowd. 'Wait a minute,' said the suddenly attentive L'Estrange. 'This happened every year?' 'Yes sir,' the guide beamed, 'every year at the solstice.' 'And the victim had to be a virgin, right?' continued L'Estrange. 'Oh yes sir,' said the guide. 'Always a virgin, untouched by man.' L'Estrange looked both puzzled and faintly disgusted. 'Geez,' he said, 'you'd think after a few years the girls would have got the message.'

Apart from this insight L'Estrange had a worry; he was afraid he was developing a drinking problem, so he too went to seek medical advice. As one does, he confessed to about half his actual intake, which was spectacular enough, but the medico was reassuring, perhaps recalling a wise remark another quack once made to me: an alcoholic can be defined as anyone who drinks more than his doctor. After a brief examination, L'Estrange was quizzed about symptoms. Did he ever drink so much that he fell over and couldn't get up again? Well yes, said L'Estrange, this had been known to happen. And after quite a lot of drinks, did he ever actually throw up? L'Estrange admitted that from time to time this had in fact been the case. Ah, said the medico, now we come to the key question. After falling over and being unable to rise, and also feeling the urge to vomit, did he have the foresight to turn onto his side before chundering? L'Estrange affirmed triumphantly that this was usually so; whereupon the medico slapped him on the back, assured him that he had no problems at all, and suggested that they go down to the pub and sort out the fee in twenty or thirty quick ones.

Unhappily the story didn't end there. A few weeks later L'Estrange, after a prolonged bout of cheap white wine, felt the need to take off all his clothes and sing. Unfortunately he was in the lobby of the Victorian Parliament House at the time, and when eventually apprehended was handed over to the men in white coats with the big butterfly nets, who took him off to a room with soft walls and removed all sharp implements from his possession. But even then there was a more or less happy ending. Upon his release L'Estrange set out on a new career and formed a right-wing speakers forum he christened The Churchill Forum – whether as a tribute to the great Tory leader's wartime oratory or to his immense capacity for booze was never made clear. It quickly went broke for lack of patronage, but at least L'Estrange had finally found his vocation.

This cautionary tale probably lacks a true moral – rather like politics in general. But it at least illustrates the need to occasionally take stock, and I don't mean the stuff that comes in those funny-shaped bottles. A reputation as the drinking champion of Parliament House is certainly better than no reputation at all, but there are more rewarding and enduring forms of notoriety for the real dreamer to aspire to. And remember, at the top, you not only meet a superior type of lush; you also get access to the parliamentary wine cellar with its unparalleled collection of Grange Hermitage, not to mention more exotic drops. It is not worth ruining your palate in the meantime.

Best wishes as always from your only mildly inebriated uncle, *Mungo*.

TWELVE

In which Jack is instructed on how to utilise
and enjoy his time on the backbench

My Dear Jack,

Having taken possession of your new office, seat in the house and swag of entitlements, you may now feel it is time to sit back and enjoy it for a while. After all, you have spent a fair time and a lot of money (mainly, it is to be hoped, other people's) getting this far. Surely it's half-time in your career; at least there should be a break to suck an orange.

But as your self-appointed coach, let me assure you that this is not the case. Far from giving you a breathing space your arrival in Canberra is a signal to redouble (at least) your efforts. If you have not made at least some kind of a mark in the next three years or before the next election (and it could come sooner) you will be typecast forever as an also-ran, at best a diligent plodder who has made his home on the back-bench and is content never to leave it. This is precisely the image we left behind with Terence Dobbin; it will never do for dynamic Jack Bentley.

You may be surprised at how many opportunities you can find to distinguish yourself. The first step, as mentioned already, is to make yourself known to the media. Did I just say make yourself known? No, ingratiate yourself, flatter and seduce and schmooze. Seek out the company of even the

159

drunkest, stupidest and most self-important of them, and don't restrict yourself to commercial television commentators. The point of contact used to be the non-members' bar; but since that venerable institution closed for want of customers (these days every office has its own bar) the National Press Club is a good second-best. Arrange to take out membership immediately; attend after-hours drinking sessions and, wherever possible, televised lunches. As in the old days when you were working your electorate, the important thing is to be seen and recognised. For many journalists the mere fact that they can remember your name will be a sign that you are an up-and-comer and perhaps even earn you a mention in dispatches, which will in turn bring you to the attention of the party heavies. As soon as you become Jack Bentley rather than Thingo, the member for Whatsisname, you will know you are on track.

You will also be expected, nay required, to put your name down for various committees, both those of the party (which examine policy questions on behalf of the membership) and parliamentary (which check out legislation before it is debated in the house). These latter have the power to call witnesses and hold public hearings, and so can become serious power bases, not to mention platforms for political drama queens such as Bronwyn Bishop – her reputation, such as it was, rested almost entirely on the fact that she was appallingly rude to bureaucrats from the Taxation Office on television. You are unlikely to reach that level of notoriety in the early days and probably shouldn't try; similarly you are not yet ready to assume the mantle of Perry Mason so successfully worn by Labor's Robert Ray and John Faulkner.

But it is important to establish a presence, so choose your committee carefully. Foreign affairs may sound glamorous, but it is also crowded; every politician ever born imagines that he is an expert on foreign policy, because it can be considered in a broad sweep rather than in the tiresome detail demanded by domestic matters. But it is out of this domestic nitty-gritty that the best political scandals emerge; many an opposition backbencher has leapt to prominence through digging away at the method by which funds are allocated by the various ministers and uncovering seeming discrepancies. Peter Costello, a genuine high flyer, got his first big break through what was called the sports rorts affair; Hawke's minister Ros Kelly was eventually trapped into admitting that she and her staff distributed tens of millions of dollars to various sporting organisations by writing applications on 'a great big whiteboard' and then ticking off the winners. Since a sizeable number of winners were in marginal Labor electorates, the feeling was that Kelly's methodology was just a fraction too casual and after a long and damaging defence she was forced to resign.

But the discrepancies only came up after Costello's dogged pursuit of her and her department through every available document; it was undoubtedly a tedious procedure, but the reward of a ministerial scalp – just about the ultimate political prize – made it all worthwhile. In any operation as large as that of the federal government there are always going to be anomalies, mistakes and peccadilloes. The trick is to incite so much public (or at least media) outrage about them that the government has eventually to cut its losses rather than risk continued political damage.

This is more likely to happen if the minister involved is (a) weak and (b) expendable. When John Howard set up his Code of Ministerial Conduct he was, at first, quite happy to apply it stringently to sack junior ministers who violated its letter. Later, when more senior ministers drove horses and carts through it, they survived because their dismissal would have been seen as too great a defeat – it was less costly to wear the stigma than chop it out. So when you start your chase after a malefactor, pick out your victim; the skilled hunter will always take the weakest member of the herd first.

Of course if you are on the government side the task becomes one of defence, but remember the best form of defence is always to counterattack. If your side is getting a pasting during a committee hearing attempt to show firstly that the members on the other side behaved in a still more unsavoury fashion when they were in government and second that their scurrilous attacks on your minister are motivated purely by spite, envy, the tall poppy syndrome and, if the worst comes to the worst, that they are soft on border protection and aiding the cause of international terrorism, or whatever happens to be the fashionable bogyman of the time. This may not get you off the hook, but it should cause enough confusion to ensure that the trouble at least spreads into the opposition ranks as well.

Another area in which you can hope to make an early impression is with your maiden speech. This is usually a routine affair during which you introduce yourself to your colleagues (well, to those of them who can be bothered to attend), explain that your electorate is probably the most beautiful, interesting and downright nice place in the whole of Australia if not on God's green earth, thank those who voted for you, promise that you will look after those who didn't as well and conclude with a few platitudes about the need to govern in the broad interests of the country for the sake of all Australians and our children (remember that bit?).

Tedious as the ritual is, it is probably best not to depart from it too far; the most extreme example was that of Edward St John who in 1967 used his maiden speech to rip into the government of which he was supposedly a member, accusing it of a cover-up over a naval disaster involving the aircraft carrier HMAS *Melbourne* and the destroyer HMAS *Voyager*. Maiden speeches are traditionally heard in silence; such was St John's vehemence that Prime Minister Harold Holt himself was moved to interject: 'That's not true.' St John paused in his diatribe for long enough to respond icily: 'I did not expect to be interrupted by the prime minister' before returning to the attack. The speech certainly got him noticed; indeed, it eventually resulted in a new inquiry into the disaster, which vindicated St John on a number of his charges. But it also marked him down as a maverick, a loose cannon, and one who was prepared to put his own concerns above those of his party. Later he was to confirm this judgement by attacking another prime minister, John Gorton, over his personal behaviour. But he had already burned his bridges; after that maiden speech no prime minister was ever going to trust St John with a ministry, whatever his genuine talents.

So don't go in there with all guns blazing. And don't try to summarise the story of your life with all its hopes and dreams in the brief time available to you, which is what

Andrew Jones did, breaking all speed-reading records and giving the Hansard reporters writer's cramp in the process. But you can liven things up a little. Try an anecdote – perhaps something amusing about your campaign, or better still a heart-rending story of injustice you will spend your political career trying to remedy. Throw in a few allusions to the political greats in your party's past, a sure method of convincing others of your dedication. Make a few friendly but pointed remarks about the inadequacies of those opposite, but don't provoke them too far at this stage – there will be plenty of time when you have settled in. And finish with a modest but specific call to arms – the old line about your hatred of cruelty to children and animals will do well enough.

You want to be seen as a man with a purpose, but not as some kind of wild-eyed crusader – someone with ideas and ability, but not too pushy. You will in any case be received with a polite chorus of 'hear hear,' but if you can arrange to be congratulated publicly by one or more of your colleagues (a favour you will of course promise to reciprocate) so much the better. And of course, alert the media. What you say will not in itself be news, but if you can provide something a bit out of the ordinary it will again mark you out as someone above the pack.

This is only the first of many speeches you will make in the course of your career, the first of many points you are going to score. Some will be easier than others; some, indeed, will be downright cheap. I have no doubt you have watched and listened to many debates in the house which are not merely rowdy but puerile. To the outsider they can be squirmingly embarrassing; how, you may ask, do these loudmouthed buffoons manage to keep a straight face? Who do they think they're impressing? The answer is all too simple: they are performing not for the discerning public, but for each other. Their immediate future lies not in the hands of the voters – the voters only get a say every three years or so, and that say does not include who will be in the ministry or even who will become the head of government. These are matters for the party room alone.

It is of course pleasant to win the approval of the mob, and better still to receive a favourable press; these things are noticed and can contribute to your standing within the party. But they are no substitute for the applause and approbation of your colleagues and in particular your leader. Deals, flattery, threats and promises are part of the process, certainly; do not flinch from any opportunity to scheme and plot, however sordid or demeaning it may appear. But a good performance on the floor of the house, especially one that ridicules and humiliates your opponents, is the surest of all methods of advancement, and certainly the most satisfying. It doesn't matter in the least if you come over as a graceless and immature smartarse to the world at large as long as you get a pat on the back from your peers. How else can one account for the advancement of someone like Tony Abbott? He certainly didn't get where he is by being kind to dogs and children.

Abbott is also a role model in another sense: he knows how to ingratiate himself with his leader. Eventually, of course, he (and you) will have to mount a challenge to the leader of the time, but at this relatively early stage it pays to keep on side. In the Liberal Party the leader in theory appoints his own ministry, although in practice he has to take account of state, gender and age balance and at least pay lip-service to the different shades of opinion inside the party room. In the Labor Party the ministry is theoretically appointed by a vote of the caucus, although in practice the leader can usually nominate people he particularly wants either in or out. The leader is thus the most influential single figure in deciding your fate: be nice to him. Study his obsessions; leaders like those they can converse with on their own terms. With Gough Whitlam a nodding acquaintance with Latin and Greek, European history and the constitution was a decided advantage. With John Howard it's cricket, the music of the 1950s, and, er, more cricket. Pander to their political priorities; more than one young minister advanced under Whitlam by showing an interest in the arts and suburban sewage, while it might not be coincidental that Abbott is, for the moment at least, a monarchist who takes a tough line on drugs. Even before making it into the ministry you can become one of the inner group, the magic circle which has access to the leader and his thinking; in short, a touch of real political power.

And don't be afraid of showing a bit of ambition, even in the first year. It is never too early to take the first step, because there will inevitably be many of them before you reach the top. In the lead-up to the 1972 election an English television interviewer named David Frost asked Prime Minister Bill McMahon and his challenger Gough Whitlam what they most admired about each other. McMahon, as was his custom, dithered, and eventually said ungraciously that he couldn't think of anything much he admired about Whitlam. But Whitlam didn't hesitate about McMahon: 'His persistence,' he replied immediately.

What Whitlam meant was that despite all the setbacks McMahon had never wavered in his single-minded purpose; he was going to be prime minister, and he was going to keep standing for the job until eventually he got it. And of course eventually he did; he saw off all the other serious contenders from the Menzies era – men of far greater ability such as Paul Hasluck, Allen Fairhall, Harold Holt, and even, finally, John Gorton. He got the job not because anyone thought he had much to offer, but because he was the last man standing – through sheer persistence. By thrusting himself forward at every available opportunity he produced a sense of inevitability about the idea that he would one day get there, and nothing was going to stop him.

His successor as Liberal leader, Billy Snedden, followed much the same path, albeit somewhat less manically. He stood for the leadership as early as 1968, having been in parliament for over 12 years but a minister for less than four of them. In spite of (or perhaps because of) a stirring endorsement written by his friend and former PR man Don Chipp which compared him to the younger Pitt and announced that he was on the wavelength of his generation, he received just two votes – presumably his own and Chipp's. Undeterred, he continued to stand as both leader and deputy at every opportunity, once again conveying the idea that a successful outcome was inevitable. When McMahon retired, there was a feeling that it would be unfair to opt for anyone other than Snedden; after all, by standing so often, he had made it his turn.

Before you get too carried away and throw your hat in the leadership ring the next chance that comes, let me add that neither McMahon nor Snedden was exactly a resounding success; the former fought and lost just one election and resigned in ignominy and the latter fought and lost just one election and was tossed out by his own party. Persistence by itself is not enough.

But it certainly helps. Just look at another last man standing, John Howard. A lesser politician – or indeed anyone with any alternative career interest at all – would have chucked it in years before he became the last, worst hope of his party. But unlike McMahon or Snedden he got the job at the right time in the political cycle, when the government was already doomed. That he held on to it for another two elections again says much for his persistence; it could be argued that opposition leader Kim Beazley, like Howard's contemporary and rival Andrew Peacock, never hungered for the job sufficiently to take it away from him. In this sense Howard remains the archetypal megalomaniac, and you have much to learn from him, not least that if the flame of ambition burns sufficiently bright, it can compensate for intellectual, emotional and moral deficiencies which would prove fatal in the more humdrum fields of human endeavour.

By now you should be seeing yourself as someone to whom normal standards no longer apply, one of those chosen not just by the people but by some greater force as a leader of men, one whose destiny is to rule over the mob, to guide it along the paths you have infallibly selected as the only correct ones. And if those paths coincide more often than not with those indicated by the opinion polls, this is no more than a fortunate coincidence; great politicians are born with the kind of clairvoyance that leads them to identify with their people and, better still, vice versa. Just as importantly, you should be seeing which of your colleagues pose the greatest threats to your own advancement and how they can best be shafted – in the national interest, of course, which by another amazing coincidence happens to be identical in every respect with your own. Louis XIV claimed that the state of France was, in fact, himself. There is no need to go to quite that extent, but it is time to make it clear that anyone interfering with the career of Jack Wentworth Bentley is, by definition, Unaustralian.

Best wishes from your staunchly, patriotically supportive uncle,
Mungo.

YOUR FIRST SPEECH

THIRTEEN

*In which we consider the rocky road
through the ministry and the risk of detours*

My Dear Jack,

Another day, another promotion.

What satisfaction it must give you to look back on the last few years and survey the trail of less fortunate, less talented and less ruthless rivals you have left behind you. Especially those you have dispatched by your own hand. There is nothing sweeter in politics than the sight of a fallen enemy with the knife in his back bearing your own fingerprints.

And, while the elimination of competitors is undoubtedly a reward in itself, and indeed almost a public duty in that politics, like any other evolutionary process, demands that the weak be culled and only the fit survive, there is the bonus; through guile, charm and the occasional political assassination you have finally forced your way onto the front bench – in government, into the ministry. Pour yourself a glass of champagne – at public expense, of course. You have well and truly earned it.

There are two ways of approaching your new responsibilities, best illustrated by example. Interestingly the two we shall choose were both ministers under Bob Hawke and both women. The sceptical might claim that this was a typical case of Hawke's attempts to ingratiate himself with sections of the public, a cynical act of tokenism or even a straightforward bid

for a root. But closer observers will have noted that both women pushed themselves up through the male pack until their colleagues were prepared to vote for them, or perhaps were afraid not to; it was, I think, Rudyard Kipling who opined that the female of the species was more deadly than the male. Be that as it may, Susan Ryan and Ros Kelly were both very tough cookies whose advancement owed little if anything to their gender.

Before Labor was elected to government in 1983 Ryan had been shadow minister for aboriginal affairs under the hapless Bill Hayden, and had played her role in the leadership struggle eventually won by Hawke. Having ended up on the winning side she claimed a reward: Ryan went to Mick Young, Hawke's close mate and adviser, and insisted that she wanted a 'real' job – apparently she felt that the advancement of indigenous Australians was still a mythical concept. Because Hawke wanted a woman in his inner cabinet (this was one time tokenism did come into play) Ryan became minister for education, a senior portfolio and a somewhat sensitive one.

Even then she was not prepared to play the game according to the old rules; when a cabinet decision went against her she took it back to the caucus and mustered the numbers to have it overturned. This was considered not only a breach of cabinet solidarity, a principle held dear by leaders because it locks in a large block of votes in times of trouble, but also a minor act of treachery. Although Ryan held her job she was no longer one of the inner circle of power and eventually resigned to pursue a profitable career in publishing and plastics. She will be remembered as Labor's first woman minister, but there was always a nagging feeling that if she had hung on and accepted the discipline for a few more years she might even have been able to transfer from the senate as Bronwyn Bishop did later and, unlike Bishop, make it all the way to the top.

Ros Kelly, by contrast, was an unashamed go-getter from day one. She announced loudly that she wanted a ministry and she didn't care what it was – she'd be happy to become minister for cats and dogs as long as it got her onto the front bench. Admirable as this honesty might have seemed, it was just a bit too blatant for her colleagues, who felt that a little more commitment to the cause would have been polite. Still, Kelly was forgiven much on the grounds that she had previously been the wife of a journalist; her lack of subtlety and couth was therefore understandable.

Hawke and Keating both took an interest in her and she was brought into the junior ministry, where she performed adequately (that is, she didn't cause any great embarrassment) before attaching herself to the Keating bandwagon in 1990. It turned out to be the right call and she became, briefly, one of the inner circle and perhaps destined by Keating for greater things. Unfortunately he did not keep a close enough eye on her, and, as previously described, her slapdash approach to grant money brought her undone. Keating tried to save her, but she had less support from the rest of the party room, which she had treated with some contempt in the past. Eventually she was forced to resign and shortly thereafter retired from politics to marry a banking mogul and settle back to the finer things in life, or at the very least shitloads of money.

So both stories have a more or less happy ending; but in

both there is the feeling of missed opportunity. What lessons does this hold for The Hon. (yes!) Jack Wentworth Bentley? First and most obviously: don't burn your bridges in the party room. You may have outshone your rivals, for the moment at least, but there will be times when you need them again. They are, after all, the people who elect the leader. Your seat in the ministry puts you in a position to dispense favours: use it. Most junior ministries afford an opportunity to do a bit of discreet pork barrelling, and unless you really make a welter of it, as did Kelly, even your opponents will accept it as a legitimate part of the game.

But cheaper and less risky is the chance to involve some at least of your colleagues in the decision-making process itself. Buy them drinks and confide snippets of not particularly secret gossip from the inside. Ask them for advice, especially on questions that may affect their own electorates. There is, of course, no compulsion to take it; you can always tell them that you have been overruled from above. But treating them as important, though not quite as important as yourself, will go some way to assuaging the spite and envy they undoubtedly feel at your success – as you used to feel about the more fortunate during your own days on the backbench.

Consulting widely also helps to avoid traps; locked away in your own little powerbase with your own little staff (and we will come to that in a minute) you can easily overlook pitfalls which would be obvious to an outsider. So rule one is: don't become isolated. Don't let power go to your head – you don't have enough of it yet to make the trip worthwhile, anyway.

As a minister you will have the right to more staff. There

is probably no need for a slave with the specific task of whispering, 'Remember, you are only mortal' in your ear when you start going over the top – which, in the early days, you probably will from time to time. But do not, repeat not, surround yourself with yes men. These are perfectly okay for your electorate staff, on whom you will now depend more than ever; your ministerial responsibilities give you a perfect excuse to turn down more tiresome invitations to fêtes, church functions and boy scout jamborees than ever, although it is wise to put in the odd appearance – never, never forget Anzac Day. But for your ministerial office, look for professionals, preferably those who have considerable knowledge of the detail of your portfolio and also a feeling for the politics of it.

Don't worry if they also happen to be smelly old drunks who look as if they have fallen off a bus and slept under a bridge; they don't have to appear much in public. Too many politicians worry about what their staff members look like. One of the great strengths of the Labor Party is, or at least used to be, that they would hire the most unlikely looking characters who hid truly prodigious talents behind horrendously scruffy exteriors. A trip through the ministerial offices in the Whitlam months, and even, though to a lesser extent, in the Hawke years, was like a tour of the Sydney City Mission after a heavy weekend. Those who worked for the coalition, however, were usually terribly pukka and often totally vacuous. Survival demands that you go for ability rather than looks.

You will also be lumbered, like it or not, with Someone From The Department; an officious shiny bum who will nominally be your liaison with the public servants under your control but whose real job will be to make sure you do as little as possible and leave the running of the country to the bureaucrats. If this evokes memories of *Yes, Minister*, then it should; life in your office will always be a constant power struggle between your political staff, who want to see you achieve and advance, and the public service, who regard you as a totally unnecessary interference in their ordered existence.

Much of your time will be spent listening to them complain about each other. Your instinct will be to side with your own appointees, and by and large this is correct, and the person from the department will expect and accept it. But don't make this person an enemy; if the department decides that you are essentially unsound, it has the capacity to make your life an utter misery. Correspondence will be lost, files will be mislaid, instructions will be misunderstood. Key officers will be unaccountably unavailable, with urgent measures unable to proceed without them. If the worst comes to the worst, your political opponents will suddenly show an extraordinary interest in your ministry and will prove to be far better informed about its shortcomings than you are yourself.

Almost the worst thing that can happen to a minister is for his department to orchestrate leaks against him. This, more than any other single factor, was responsible for the loans affair devouring the Whitlam government; Treasury, miffed at having been left out of the original plan (which it heartily disliked in any case), began to feed the opposition through a contact known as Mr Williams – later identified in the senate under privilege as Des Moore – day-by-day reports about the government's progress or lack of it, couched in terms which

made the operation appear not only incompetent, but possibly even criminal. While this is the only recent instance of a
parallel to Washington's Deep Throat, there have been many
shallower throats who have gravely embarrassed governments
from time to time – it was, for instance, a leak from the Cus-
toms Department which revealed that then Health Minister
Michael MacKellar had failed to declare the import of a
colour television set, and brought about the temporary demise
of both MacKellar himself and John Moore, the business and
consumer affairs minister who tried to cover up for him. If the
public service as a whole turns hostile, there is little you or any
of your colleagues can do about it. But you can at least make
the effort to keep your own bit of it on side.

But it is not only the department that will be playing Big
Brother; you will also be directly responsible to your senior
minister, the one who sits in cabinet on the right hand (figu-
ratively at least) of the prime minister himself. This used not
always to be the case; while some super departments had their
bureaucratic offspring (Defence, for instance, oversaw the separate divisions of Army, Navy, Air Force and Supply), most
ministries were more or less independent. But the modern
trend is to more vertical organisation. If you are lucky, your
superior will let you have your head – he may be already
happily preparing for retirement on the enormous super-
annuation to which his position entitles him, and yours is
starting to mount up as well. If you are not, he will burden you
with all the really boring stuff while keeping the plums for
himself.

One particularly grim scenario involves those areas
where you have constant pressure from some of the more

fanatical interest groups, particularly those who sneak the media in with them. It is said that upon achieving the rank of leader of the opposition, the equivalent at least of a very senior ministry, Kim Beazley told his staff that there was a new and unbreakable rule: his office was closed to women, greenies, Aborigines and gays. If they wanted to lobby the ALP they would have to go to his more junior colleagues and take their chances. This hard line enraged the groups concerned, but among insiders there was considerable sympathy for Beazley's stance: political life is too short to spend it talking to those who will never, ever be satisfied, no matter what concessions are made. This may sound a little unfair to the mainstream of all those barred by Beazley, many of whom can be quite rational for short periods, if kept away from stimulants such as disagreeing with anything they might say. But the fringe is something else again.

During the high days of feminist protest, when women wearing T-shirts bearing such encouraging slogans as 'Dead Men Don't Rape' and 'Women Who Want To Be Trucks' took over King's Hall and camped on the lawns outside, hardened members of parliament hid in the lavatories rather than risk face-to-face confrontation. I recall one shaking minister who had dared to walk through the camp to reach his office: he was told brusquely that this was 'women's space', and to clear off. He protested feebly that it was in fact public land, but beat a hasty retreat when a group of amazonian types advanced on him. From the safety of the steps of Parliament House he turned round to see one of them triumphantly raise her skirt and urinate on the spot he had occupied, marking it as her own.

These are the sort of people a malicious superior can wish on you. Comfort yourself with the knowledge that your turn will come, and also point out gently that, just as the public service can make life difficult for you, you can also cause a few niggling problems for him. But don't be too loud-mouthed about it; always remember that if this particular policy area ever requires a scapegoat, you are still a lot lower on the totem pole than he is.

Even after you have placated and, with a bit of luck and skill, tamed your departmental man and your senior minister, there is still one more danger. Within the prime minister's very office there lurks a shadowy figure who is the leader's personal adviser on matters relating to your portfolio. This idea of a government within the government was started by Malcolm Fraser, who expanded the old Prime Minister's Department to make it a sort of super ministry shadowing everything. Since then leaders from both sides have taken up the idea and even the leader of the opposition now has staff advisers on just about everything. These people can be immensely powerful; Mark Latham's resignation from Kim Beazley's shadow ministry was a result of his draft education policy being rewritten in the leader's office. The same can happen to you – not, of course, the resignation, a weapon only to be used if you believe you can bring the leader down as a result, but the note declaring your efforts null and void and substituting whatever rush of blood to the head the leader's adviser has suffered.

Unless you have made yourself one of the magic circle with access to the leader's office yourself, there isn't much you can do about this except try to tie up all your projects so tightly that it becomes more trouble than it's worth to unravel them; that, and gain public and party room support for them before the leader's office knows what's going on. To this end, keep working away at the media. Whenever you have something to announce, however trivial, hold a press conference. Do not be discouraged if no one comes; you can always put out a press release which infers that there has been tremendous interest, even if the source of it is a bit vague.

The old National Party warhorse Sir John McEwen turned this into something of an art form. His portfolio of trade, and particularly agricultural trade, was decidedly unsexy, but never a week went past without a press release beginning: 'The Deputy Prime Minister and Minister for Trade, Sir John McEwen, was asked this morning whether he could guarantee the survival of the International Wheat Agreement in the face of falling prices …' or something similar. In fact, the only person who had asked him was his press secretary. Nonetheless, McEwen's ruminations usually got a run as a result. The technique of the phantom interviewer is not one to be dismissed.

So keep, as always, pushing yourself forward. But remember, you are still to some extent on trial; your leader can thrust you off the front bench just as easily as he thrust you onto it. Vindicate his judgement by boosting yourself (and therefore the party), sucking up to him and above all keeping out of trouble. This by itself can bring unimaginable rewards.

In the run-up to the 1977 elections John Howard was a newly arrived solicitor whom Malcolm Fraser had buried in the undistinguished and short-lived portfolio of Special Trade Negotiations. In the normal course of events he would have stayed there for some time, in spite of having squirmed his way into Fraser's confidence. But then the treasurer, Phillip Lynch, suddenly found himself in the middle of a series of sordid allegations concerning shonky property dealings. He instantly disappeared into hospital citing a problem with a kidney stone (what is it about this organ which makes it so attractive to politicians in trouble?) but the media didn't let up. Fraser, caught in the middle of an election campaign, finally got tired of being asked if his treasurer was a little crook by smartarse reporters pretending to inquire about Lynch's health and decided the man had to go; and, as he cast around for a replacement among his rather shop-soiled team, there was the gnomish figure of John Howard, clean as a hound's tooth and radiating availability. And the rest is history.

You are, of course, unlikely to have luck like that; but for the moment at least, keep yourself nice. There will be plenty of time for a bit of rough trade later.

Fond regards from your grasping uncle,
Mungo.

FOURTEEN

In which Uncle Mungo describes the sport of bare-knuckle oratory and its potential rewards

My Dear Jack,

In re-reading my last letter to you it occurs to me that I have been unnecessarily grim about your life as a minister. I have spent too much time on what should be avoided rather than what can be enjoyed. Let me correct this at once. Even in the junior ranks (and we trust you will only occupy them for a short time before continuing your now-inevitable ascendancy) there are many opportunities for self-indulgence, domination and most of the other more pleasurable vices.

I have already quoted that great war criminal and vulgarian, Henry Kissinger, on the efficacy of power as an aphrodisiac; now is the time to put it to the test, although a little discretion is advisable. Even Bob Hawke in his pre-parliamentary days had the occasional knock-back, and he was certainly a far more powerful figure than any junior minister. There was the celebrated occasion in 1971 on which he appeared, somewhat tired and emotional, on the doorstep of a Sydney socialite whose Labor sympathies were well known – indeed, notorious. 'How would you like,' slurred the then president of the ACTU, ostentatiously depositing an overnight bag at her feet, 'to be the mistress of the next prime minister of Australia?' To her great credit, his intended victim did not miss a beat. 'Oh,' she replied, 'I don't really think that Margaret Whitlam would like that,' and closed the door firmly. But it must be said that Hawke had far more hits than misses, and not a few of them were due more to his perceived political clout than to his intrinsic charm – although he had his share of that as well.

Then there are the purely material gains: access to corporate boxes for sporting events, as many free lunches as you can stomach, generally favoured treatments at public functions. Barry Cohen, a junior minister in the Hawke years, fondly recalls his first visit to the Sydney Festival's Opera in the Park as a VIP. In a special section roped off for politicians, media heavyweights and other favoured freeloaders, he was happily munching chicken and sipping champagne when an unmistakable voice assailed his earhole: 'Hey Bazza, this beats being in opposition, eh? If we were, we'd be up the back chewing on a Mars Bar.' The self-appointed cultural czar, Paul Keating, was enjoying himself too.

These occasions are to be savoured, but the real highs come on the overseas trips. On these, embassies and their staffs will be pulled off their real duties to cater to your every whim. Keating and his treasury secretary, John Stone, happened to be in New York at the time Alan Bond's syndicate won the America's Cup. While the prime minister was disporting himself in an appalling sports jacket in Perth and urging workers to celebrate by taking a day off, Keating and Stone demanded transport to Newport where they quaffed champagne before returning to the International Monetary Fund meeting, which was the ostensible purpose of their trip. To this end senior diplomats were deployed to arrange transport, accommodation and who knows what other comforts for the two roisterers.

This, after all, is what the Foreign Service is for, and it needs to be kept up to the mark. Alexander Downer was quite right to throw on a hissy fit when he arrived in some far-flung capital only to be met, not by the Mercedes he had requested – no, ordered – but by some lesser vehicle. On one celebrated occasion in the early '70s a sensitive third secretary in one of our Asian embassies failed to fulfil the request of a visiting defence minister for female company; the man was promptly transferred to a hardship posting at the end of the earth and left to rot there.

In this context it should be noted that favours of this kind need to be reciprocated. Fortunately there are now a number of brothels and call girl services in Canberra to manage the ever-growing demand, but it was not always thus. Hardened foreign affairs officials still shudder at the memory of a visit from an Asian delegation in the early '60s, who demanded a spot of relaxation at the end of a hard day's negotiating. After all, they said reasonably, they had provided any number of willing women during a visit to their homeland by Australian officials; surely it was time for a return presentation. The young bureaucrat in charge of showing them around pan-icked; he could think of nowhere in Canberra that could be trusted with the job. As the Asians grew steadily more impa-tient he rang hotels and their doormen and made inquiries from passing taxi drivers; still he drew a blank. Finally, an unsavoury-looking barman gave him an address, not in Canberra but in nearby Queanbeyan. Gleefully he piled his charges into a fleet of cabs and hurtled to the destination, to be greeted by an effusive madam. Certainly, she said, for the right price she could accommodate his eight gentlemen. But as they eagerly dismounted from the taxis her face changed. Sorry, said the madam: no coloureds.

You, of course, will never be in such an embarrassing position; pimping and pandering can be left to Australia's finest diplomats. This, after all, is their job; take full advantage. But welcome as these material perks undoubtedly are, the best thing about being on the front bench is that, for the first time in your already impressive career, you can actually concentrate on the main game: humiliating those on the other side.

You have, of course, already made your contribution; a snide interjection or two, a roar of contempt as part of the systematic destabilising of their position, riotous applause if your own speakers gain a point, and perhaps (if you are lucky enough to gain favour with the party whips) a loaded question or two, or even a brief speech. You will have also done your bit in the committee hearings, although most such efforts remain unsung unless some major scandal is afoot. But for most of the time you have been at best an enthusiastic spectator. Your main efforts have been within your own party – seeking to gain advantage over your colleagues by whatever means possible.

You have had to contend with, and kowtow to, the hard men who operate the factional systems, open or tacit, which effectively run every party. These days in fact the iron grip is loosening up; old-timers on the conservative side will tell you that you have it easy as they speak with awe of the days when Malcolm Fraser relied on his trio of National Party front row forwards, Doug Anthony, Ian Sinclair and Peter Nixon, to keep order, while over in the senate Reg 'The Toecutter' Withers ruled uncontested. Strong Labor men still quail at the name of Graham Richardson and his enforcer Leo McLeay; they were jovially known as Richo and Leaping Leo, but were more furtively compared to Arthur Daly and his minder Terry McCann. Bill Hayden, an ex-Queensland copper and no shrinking violet (despite his disconcerting habit of hiding in the cupboard of his ministerial office before bursting forth to greet his surprised visitors), used to say that being called 'mate' by this pair or any of their troops on the New South Wales Right was like getting a kiss from the mafia. He suggested that they spent their spare time tearing the wings off butterflies.

In more recent times things have been more relaxed, although there are those who would still prefer not to run into Laurie Brereton, Richo's nominal successor, on a dark night or into John Howard's somewhat unstable doppelgänger Bill Heffernan anywhere at any time. You still have to pay due regard to your party's movers and shakers; after all, they probably helped to put you where you are, or at least did not make an all-out effort to block your progress. And what they have made, they can unmake; think of the amiable Barry Cohen, Hawke's first environment minister, who was unceremoniously returned to the backbench not for any fault in his performance, but because he got offside with Richo. The party bosses demand their share of respect. But they are no longer your chief concern. While you will never be able to stop watching your back altogether, you can at least spend a bit more time focusing across the chamber and lining up those on the other side.

As a frontbencher you will be expected to play a major

role in their destruction; in return they will see you as a potential prize scalp. You will be targeted as a newcomer during question time: hit back with barely controlled violence. You will always get more points for bashing the opposition than for defending the government, and practically none for giving an honest and considered reply. Some years ago an observer from the parliamentary library rechristened question time, the 45 minutes or so allocated daily to questions without notice, 'Questions without Answers', and things have only got worse since. Question time is simply an opportunity for combat; it has as much to do with the exchange of information as does world championship wrestling. Get in there with all boots flailing.

If you have shown any talent at all for debate, or perhaps better still personal abuse (and as I remember you were always an argumentative child), you will be called on frequently to take part in the proceedings, and not only in areas relating to your portfolio. Every parliament has its hard hitters, and it pays to be one of them; as always, your first aim is to be noticed.

But you have to decide just what kind of hard hitting will be your speciality. The temptation will be to head straight for the top – to imitate the lofty style of a Menzies or a Whitlam, both great parliamentary performers who proved themselves almost invulnerable on the floor of the House of Representatives. This is indeed the stuff of which great political leaders are made. But there is a catch; it really only works if you are a leader, or at least clearly destined to follow that path. You, Jack, we hope and believe are in that mould, but perhaps it is too early to try to master the role. There have been many in the last half-century who have gone close to emulating the oratorical skills of the leaders, but have lacked that final killer touch; more often than not they have ended up as little more than footnotes. Who now recalls Harry Turner, who held Bradfield, then the safest Liberal seat in the country, for more than 20 years? On his day he was one of the best and most urbane orators from either house, but he never progressed beyond the backbench. Other fine performers did better: Kim Beazley senior and John Wheeldon were both ministers in the Whitlam government, but both are now remembered (when they are remembered at all) more for their eccentricities than for any lasting imprint on the political scene. Those at the very top can afford a certain detachment; those still on the way up must be prepared to get into the rough and tumble.

This need not be a cause of regret; like may contact sports political brawling can be not only character building but quite good fun. The great clowns of parliament – men like Labor's Fred Daly and the Liberals' Jim Killen – gave every sign of genuinely enjoying themselves as they ridiculed their opponents to the laughter and applause of, quite often, both sides of the house. Humour is a great weapon, but be wary: the politically correct thought police are poised to jump on any real or assumed mockery of their icons. Alexander Downer, having adoped as his slogan 'Things that Matter', never really recovered after describing his policy on domestic violence as 'Things that Batter'. Then there are the real bovver boys, the take-no-prisoners types like Eddie Ward or Ian Sinclair; their modern-day equivalents are of course Tony Abbott and Mark Latham. These are the ones who go for the throat: there are even times when their passion – or at least their hatred – can seem almost real. Interestingly, they usually get a bit further up the greasy totem pole than the clowns, although they are seldom greatly liked or admired by their colleagues. It was the distinctly unlovable emperor Tiberius who coined the phrase 'let them hate me as long as they fear me', and the political thugs, unlikely as they are to have read Suetonius, appear to follow this motto. Every leader needs one or two on the front bench, and often, as Abbott did, they become court favourites – for a time at least. But it is a long time since one of them has actually moved into the Lodge. The last was probably Billy Hughes, and he moved out again in 1923.

Their main function is to cause trouble and disruption, which fills page after page of the newspapers on the day after it happens and is then the subject of much pompous tut-tutting by the editorialists the day after that. I have always found there to be a largish element of humbug in all this: if they disapprove of 'inappropriate behaviour', as they choose to call it, so deeply, why then do they give it so much publicity? There is something reminiscent of the football commentators who sanctimoniously deplore any form of violence in the game on the grounds that it turns the mums and the kiddies away, and then foam at the mouth and scream for claret at the first sign of an actual blue developing. The editorial lines are similar: all this rowdiness and larrikinism frightens children and causes the punters to become cynical and disillusioned about the parliamentary process. But by golly it's good copy.

It has apparently escaped these pundits that a large major-ity of Australians have been disillusioned with the political process since the year dot, and at the very worst a spot of biffo during question time will only confirm them in their views. Indeed, they find the sight of politicians being polite to each

other hypocritical, if not downright nauseating; their instinct is to urge them to get on with it, get stuck into each other. They see politics for what it is: conflict, battle, war – war without blood, perhaps, but then, as von Clausewitz pointed out, war is nothing more than the continuation of politics by other means. Think of the money we are saving by keeping all the aggro within the bounds of Parliament House.

Moreover, if the public was really going to be turned off the political process by the occasional stoush it would have happened long ago. Whatever bitterness there is these days is a mere shadow of what happened back in 1909, when Alfred Deakin's Protectionist Party, which had supported Andrew Fisher's minority Labor government, decided to merge with the Freetraders under Joseph Cook to form the conservative anti-Labor alliance which has shaped Australian politics ever since. Sir William Lyne, who stayed loyal to Labor, shouted at Deakin: 'Judas! Judas! Judas!' Labor's Billy Hughes replied mildly: 'I do not agree with that; it is not fair to Judas, for whom there is this to be said, that he did not gag the man whom he betrayed, nor did he fail to hang himself afterwards.' On another occasion Hughes's invective enraged Deakin to the point where the prime minister interjected: 'I deny it! I deny it! I deny it!' There was silence; the speaker asked Hughes if he had finished his speech, to which Hughes replied: 'Oh no, Mr Speaker, I was just waiting for the cock to crow.' Deakin, who in spite of his nickname Affable Alfred was also able to turn an insult back on Hughes: 'He presents as undignified a spectacle as the ill-bred urchin one sees dragged from a tart shop kicking and screaming as he goes.' The rows went on: it was, Labor threatened, to be a war to the knife with a stiletto finish. One all-night session in which the invective was more than usually vigorous was too much for the speaker, Sir Frederick Holder. With a last mutter of 'Dreadful, dreadful' he fell out of his chair and was dead before breakfast.

But even this was tame stuff compared to the colonial parliaments of the nineteenth century. In the New South Wales Legislative Assembly in 1886 a debate on the innocuous subject of tariffs produced amazing scenes. One member took possession of the table, shouting, 'There is no house, and we are a rabble.' Another crowed like a cock. Attempts by the speaker to restore order were greeted with cries of 'Damn the chair!' When an opposition member attempted to speak the premier, Sir Henry Parkes, rushed at him, shook a threatening fist and shouted: 'You damned bugger, you Fenian – who are you?' Indeed, things frequently became physical, particularly late at night when the members were more than usually tired and emotional. The magazine *Table Talk* reports one occasion when 'members simply knocked the stuffing out of each other and kicked each other in a most sacred part'. One member suggested, not altogether in jest, the erection of a 24-foot boxing ring within the house for the more convenient settlement of honourable gentlemen's disputes, which would at least save the cost of regularly replacing the house crockery. It would seem fairly clear that if Australians had really been as sensitive and squeamish about political brawling as the delicate plants who write the editorials believe, we would never even have got as far as federation, let alone more than a century of unbroken parliamentary government.

So do not take too much notice of the shrieks of dismay that emanate from the media; if they were serious they would not devote so much space to reporting the so-called disgraceful behaviour in the first place. But remember also that unmitigated aggression is not enough by itself. Even Billy Hughes had a flashing sense of wit, as can be seen from the exchanges noted above. Paul Keating, reviled by his opponents as one of the more ruthless and foul-mouthed players of the modern era, could also be both funny and charming when he chose, as he put it, to throw the switch to vaudeville. John Howard lacks that kind of easy mastery; in full flight he sounds like nothing so much as an aggrieved duck. But no one has ever accused him of lack of toughness.

The knack, of course, is to have a whole array of styles in your repertoire and to use the one most appropriate to the occasion – but with the big stick always at hand for emergencies. Think of each speech as a seduction; with sufficient practice you will generally be able to charm your victims into submission. And if you can't, you can always threaten to break both their arms.

Your excited, if politically incorrect, uncle,
Mungo.

FIFTEEN

*In which Jack receives his final instructions
before preparing for the summit*

My Dear Jack,

At last, it's time — or at any rate the countdown has begun. You are now a senior minister recognised among your peers as a serious player. The next step, the penultimate slither towards the top of the greasy totem pole, is to persuade them that you are a contender, or better still, the obvious successor. The final confirmation of your impending triumph will come when respectable media commentators start referring to you as 'the heir apparent'.

But even so close to the summit, there is still work to do. By now your rivals are far fewer, but they are even more intense than the has-beens you have seen off during your relentless rise. Take stock of them, as they undoubtedly are taking stock of you. Look around the cabinet room — it is from there that the challenges will generally come. There are, of course, cases of outsiders being proposed — in recent years the conservatives have toyed with such absurdities as Joh Bjelke-Petersen, Bronwyn Bishop, even the bully-boy businessman John Elliott whom, incredibly, one group of conspirators wanted to import into parliament and the leadership at the very time he was about to face trial. But these were desperate times; Andrew Peacock and John Howard were both proven losers, and the immediate substitutes – John Hewson and, finally, Alexander Downer – proved to be no better. Still, even they were seen as superior to the proven failure of Howard, who was literally the last card in the pack.

Labor has had similar flirtations; when Bill Hayden seemed to be taking them nowhere there were suggestions that Neville Wran be wooed from New South Wales; eventually, of course, Bob Hawke stepped into the vacuum, although many of his colleagues had grave reservations about his lack of parliamentary experience and his overcharged ego (not to mention libido and thirst). But these outsiders and blow-ins only got their chance because there was no obvious successor – no heir apparent. The trick is to manoeuvre yourself into that role so that if anything happens to your beloved leader, either physically or politically, you are the automatic choice.

It can help if the leader himself anoints you; this makes for an easy transition when the time comes, and few will have the temerity to challenge the leader's judgement and try to organise a counter-coup against you, at least for a while. The drawback is that it also makes it very difficult, though not impossible, for you to challenge the leader; you have to wait until he is ready to go in his own sweet time, and this can be dispiriting. Indeed, your leader may decide to hang on until the very moment that defeat appears inevitable, and then graciously pass to you what has become known as the poisoned chalice.

An exception to this rule was the retirement of Sir Robert Menzies in 1966, still held up as a model by leaders who believe they should have the right to nominate their own use-by date. When Menzies eventually stepped aside, he had been there far too long and his party had long since run out of both energy and ideas – there was no way it was ever going to recapture what the old man referred to wistfully as 'that first, fine, careless rapture'. But on the other hand, the Labor opposition was still a mess, under the control of the two-time loser Arthur Calwell, with Gough Whitlam and his great reform agenda caught behind the succession barrier. Menzies, having disposed of all the serious contenders who might have become rivals to himself (a technique you should study and refine for the time of your own ascension), anointed the amiable Harold Holt, a politician of unquestioned loyalty but remarkable shallowness. Still, it was at a time when Holt was able to establish himself sufficiently to take on the bitter and ageing Calwell, and in the wash-up the Liberals won not one but two more elections before the inevitable crash, which, when it came, was so far down the track that no one could possibly blame Menzies – although it was his 17-year tenure which effectively sucked the verve and talent out of the party.

The case of Bob Hawke and Paul Keating provides the reverse example. In spite of what Keating at least saw as a solemn agreement, Hawke refused to go when his time was up and spent much of his last term fighting a debilitating battle which he eventually lost, but which left the party all but exhausted. When Keating finally won the election that followed, a win due almost entirely to the incompetence of the coalition in general and its leader John Hewson in particular, Labor was already on borrowed time. It says much for Keating's determination that he was able to snatch another three years, but it was not what he had planned and wanted.

You, of course, deserve better. Set your course accordingly. First, have a look at your senior colleagues. How many of them really, truly, want to be prime minister? The answer may shock you. A surprising – to my mind alarming – number of politicians are satisfied with a secondary role. They want to get close enough to the top to administer large departments, to oversee change in their chosen field, but they are not ready for the ultimate responsibility. Consider, for example, the line-up after Holt went under the waves at the end of 1967. The times were admittedly not ideal; by then Whitlam was on the rise and even some coalition supporters were saying that it was time for the conservatives to take a short break in opposition. But this would not have deterred a man of real political ambition, particularly one bred to consider government as his natural right.

However, the only one who was prepared to get in there and fight for it was Billy McMahon, and he was promptly put out of the race through a thunderous veto from the Country Party leader Jack McEwen, rather to the relief of many of McMahon's fellow Liberals. Paul Hasluck thought the job should be his by right of superior intellect, but he wasn't interested enough to actually campaign for it. Allen Fairhall, the other most senior Liberal, was quite happy to stick with a quiet life in the general area of defence; he did not even put his hand up. David Fairbairn was only ever there from a sense of duty; his wife wanted him to be prime minister but he didn't. Les Bury was persuaded to run by the Sydney business community, who wanted one of their own for the job, but was clearly out of his depth and stayed largely in the background. The young and brash Bill Snedden threw his hat in the ring, but only as an indication that he was seeking advancement in the longer term. It was this lack of enthusiasm as much as a dissatisfaction with the talent available that caused the young Turks of the Liberal Party to drag in Jolly John Gorton from the senate; at least he looked as if he would enjoy the job, as indeed he did. The point is that any reasonably dynamic minister who had kept McEwen on side and was prepared to go out and sell himself to the troops would have waltzed into the Lodge at the beginning of 1968, and who knows what might have happened then?

Again, after the disaster of 1975, Whitlam was prepared to hand over immediately to Bill Hayden, but Hayden had doubts; he went off to finish a university degree instead. When he finally decided he was ready Whitlam had had second thoughts and hung on until 1977. If Hayden had jumped earlier he might well have established himself in the first couple of years, picked up a few seats at the next election and been in a position to win at the one after. The moral of these stories is easy: never let a chance go by. Some times may be better than others at which to take over the leadership, but there is never a time so bad that you should let it slip on the grounds that there will always be another chance. It may never come and if it does you will have lost nothing by grabbing it early. Look, not for the first or last time, at John Howard.

As for preparation: this is largely a matter of perception. Ideally, of course, you will have served in a variety of ministries, up to and including the treasury: indeed, a spell as treasurer has sometimes been thought to be both a necessary and sufficient condition to succeed as prime minister. We

now know, of course, that this is a complete furphy. If some of the best prime ministers have indeed been former treasurers (Chifley springs to mind) so have some of the worst (McMahon). Others have made a fair fist of the job without having gone anywhere near treasury: Curtin, Menzies, Whitlam, Fraser, Hawke … the idea that the experience of treasury and its particular brand of economics is essential training for the good governance of the nation is very much an invention of treasury itself and its supporters among the econocrats.

And of course, should you become prime minister by winning an election from opposition, you may never have had a chance to enjoy the keys to the vault. Of the five post-war PMs to achieve office in this manner only one – Howard – has been a former treasurer. So forget that line, although of course, if a spell as treasurer offers, you would be mad to knock it back. The main thing you need is simply loads of ambition and a positive glow of self-confidence, up to and including a touch of arrogance. If your colleagues are convinced that you are ready for the job, that you know what you are doing and that, above all, you are the type who can win elections and therefore provide goodies for them as well as for yourself, they will follow.

And now for the nitty-gritty. For most of your career you will have been a loyal supporter of your leader, whoever he happens to be. This will always win you brownie points, even when your leader is demonstrably hopeless. The only possible exception to the rule is when it becomes obvious that your leader is doomed, and that the challenger unquestionably has the numbers. You may then say that, in the interests of party

solidarity and to avoid ongoing division and bitterness, you will throw your weight and that of your supporters (mythical or otherwise) behind the new order – always bearing in mind the true, if cynical, adage: Treason doth never prosper – what's the reason? For if it prosper, none dare call it treason. Even in the 16th century, Sir John Harington knew his politics.

Your conspicuous loyalty to your leader (or leaders, as is more frequently the case) has been a factor in your advancement, perhaps even in your role as his chosen successor. Be aware, however, that this in itself may not be enough. Not all leaders get the successor they want; even the formidable Jack McEwen was unable to persuade the Country Party of the talents of the urbane Ian Sinclair over those of the more rustic Doug Anthony. But anointed or not, the time will probably come when you need to mount a formal challenge.

The first step in the process is to make sure you have at least a small clique of supporters of your own. Promise them whatever they ask for – ministries, ambassadorships, appointments to the High Court, even the governor-generalship, although it is best not to promise too many of them the same job in case they compare notes. Sadly there is now less largesse available than there used to be; the pernicious process of privatisation has severely curtailed patronage. No longer can a plum job on the Qantas board be held out as the ultimate reward. But do not despair; there are still obscure positions such as the War Graves Commission, postings that involve unlimited luxury travel combined with very little work. Some of your less ambitious colleagues who are in politics for a good time rather than for a long time will jump at the chance of such glittering prizes. Do not hesitate to cash in on their greed; and, if at the end of the day you, like Richard III and other great political operators of the past, fail to deliver, well, there's not really all that much they can do about it until next time, and you are in the best position to ensure that there won't be a next time.

Having secured your power base, use it to start undermining your current leader. There is no need to be too specific; the mere suggestion that he perhaps treats the job a bit lightly, that his best days are past him, that he may no longer have quite what it takes, that some in the electorate are starting to see him as a loser – this is really all it takes to start things off. As the word circulates, others will be drawn in; they will begin to interpret everything he does as a possible setback to their own careers. What were once laughed off as minor errors will assume greater significance; eventually they will be seen as part of a pattern of political incompetence rather than the normal hiccups any administration, no matter how well run, is bound to experience.

Now is the time to introduce lines like, 'When you think about it, it's really not all that long till the next election. We must do something to get our act together.' Of course, never even hint at the idea that you yourself might be running for leader. Leave that to others. When they bring it up, shrug it aside: 'Oh, that's absurdly hypothetical. Of course the leader (best not to mention his name here) has my full support. I mean, if the party actually felt it needed me in any position, I'd do my best to help …' This is really all that's required. The media, ever alert to the faintest possibility of a leadership challenge, will pick it up and run straight away. By now you will of course have cultivated a few key journalists in whom you can confide: 'Of course this is strictly off the record, but I'm afraid our leader just hasn't got it any more. He'll have to go – it's not a matter of if, it's a matter of when. He's political dead meat.' Expect to see this faithfully reproduced in learned commentaries, and not just those of the reporters to whom you have spoken. You can also speak mysteriously about 'internal polling', which may mean nothing more than a chat in the bar with selected colleagues but sounds terribly grand. The implication is there is an overwhelming public demand for you, as opposed to the incumbent – you are the Bob Hawke to his Bill Hayden. Actually, of course, there has never been an overwhelming public demand for any politician living or dead – the mere idea is derisory. But it is amazing what journalists will believe, especially if you have a page of bodgie figures to back it up. The game, as they say, is now afoot. The media, your political allies and your own instincts will tell you when it is time to trigger a crisis.

History shows that one of the best ways to do this is a statesmanlike speech on the subject of leadership, or rather the current, sad, lack of it in Australia. A fine example of this took place in 1938, as the young Bob Menzies was attempting to knock off the United Australia Party Prime Minister Joe Lyons. Menzies constantly queried the course the party was taking, suggesting that more of a sense of purpose and direction was needed. Lyons himself, a former Labor man who had been poached by the Tories as an avuncular vote catcher, never really took much notice; but his wife Enid, a far more accomplished politician, saw what was going on and blew the whistle loudly and often.

Menzies then took what can be seen as the logical next

step in a challenge; he resigned from the ministry over what he maintained were policy differences, principally with the Country Party leader Earle Page. Resignation is the crossing of the Rubicon, the last throw of the dice, and should only ever be used as part of a leadership challenge – certainly never, ever, in a fit of pique or a matter of principle. Labor's amiable aboriginal affairs spokesman, Daryl Melham, did the latter and disappeared without a trace, despised by his colleagues as a wimpy idealist. The normal course would have been for Menzies to build support and take Lyons head-on in the party room; in fact Lyons died before this development could take place and Menzies succeeded him in spite of Page's attempts to impose a veto.

More than 50 years later, Paul Keating's challenge to Bob Hawke took a very similar form. There was the speech to the press gallery in which he deplored the lack of great leaders in Australia while comparing himself to the master tenor Placido Domingo; then the first, failed bid, followed by resignation from the ministry and regrouping on the backbench; then the final blow. With minor variations (the speech on leadership sometimes comes after the resignation rather than before it, and the time spent on the backbench does not always result in a fresh challenge; Andrew Peacock never risked a second crack at Malcolm Fraser) the pattern is generally the same.

The key to success is to choose your moment for the first strike carefully, when there is some momentum with you; but even then be prepared to lose. First strikes are seldom successful, even when the superiority of the challenger is obvious to all. It took Malcolm Fraser two goes to knock off Billy

Snedden and Bob Hawke lost to Bill Hayden once before Hayden threw in the towel with the numbers overwhelmingly against him. One reason is that the leader usually has the built-in support of most of his front bench and those in other party positions; after all, to an extent they are dependent on his patronage. As these usually constitute the largest single block in the party room, the cautious will tend to side with them. The inertia that goes with incumbency is another thing; parties are unwilling to change horses because to do so means having to start all over again to establish a new ministry and a different attack on the opposition; they have to admit that they were wrong last time around and that the time since has been largely wasted.

But do not be discouraged. Unless the challenger is utterly routed at the first try (as happened with Peacock and Fraser) everyone knows that nothing has really been settled; the divisions have been opened up, and the challenger, who now has nothing to lose, will continue to attack until he wins. After the first attempt the party is half-paralysed anyway; the leader's energy is diverted from his opponents on the other side of the house to those sitting behind him. Eventually the political cost becomes too much; waverers realise that the fight can really only have one outcome and change their allegiance. And then, my boy, we have a new leader.

You are nearly there – so close to the Lodge that I can almost smell the reek of those awful cigars, which Hawke used to smoke and have left their redolence in the upholstery. So once more into the breach, dear Jack – stiffen the sinews, summon up the blood and imitate the action of the tiger, or at least of the striking scorpion which, if rather less attractive, is also a far more efficient predator.

Tarantara from your victory-scenting uncle,
Mungo.

SIXTEEN

*In which Uncle Mungo and Jack rejoice
at the latter's ascension and prepare to enjoy it*

My Dear, Dear Jack,

Oh frabjous day, callooh, callay, the morning's at seven, the hillside's dew-pearled, Jack's in the Lodge and all's right with the world. Jack Wentworth Bentley PM — I always knew you had it in you and now you're in it.

But do not relax for a moment. Now, while the cheers are still ringing in your ears and the opposition and the media are drunk, demoralised and exhausted, is the time to act. Is there something outrageous, something thoroughly unconscionable, that you wish to do? Do it now.

It was at this moment in his career that John Howard announced casually that rather than move to Canberra he planned to take over Kirribilli House, the Sydney harbourside mansion previously available to prime ministers only when it was not being used by visiting VIPs. The ostensible reason? As a good family man he wanted to be near his son during his last year at school. Six years later the Howard family was scattered across the face of the earth, although still funded by taxpayers for everything from parking fees to conducted tours of Paris. But John and (especially) Janette were still ensconced at Kirribilli, and it would have taken several tonnes of high explosive to remove them.

This was grand larceny on an epic scale: a theft of public property that would have made Ronald Biggs envious. But Howard received far less criticism for his audacious robbery than Paul Keating had received a couple of years earlier for his purchase of a new dining table for the Lodge. It's all in the timing. Seize the day; it will be a long time before you can act in such an untrammelled fashion again.

There is an old joke about the prime minister who, on coming to office, finds that his predecessor has left him three envelopes, to be opened in order in the event of a major political crisis. After a few months the first disaster strikes; the PM opens the first envelope and finds the advice: 'Blame your predecessors.' So he gets stuck into the opposition for its terrible failures and the mess it has left behind for his government to clean up, and it works; things return to normal. Then a bit further down the track comes a new predicament; the second envelope suggests: 'Blame the media.' So he lambasts the press, radio and television for their bias, their incompetence and their inability to report what really matters; and again things settle down. But once again an emergency looms, so the PM confidently opens the last envelope. This time the message is stark: 'Prepare three envelopes.'

It makes a nice story, but it's manifestly untrue; if it weren't, very few governments in Australia would survive their first year. For starters, there are many more scapegoats around than just the opposition and the media, and all of them can be used more than once. Over the years the Westminster system, under which ministers take responsibility for their departments and the prime minister takes overall responsibility for the government, has been eroded to vanishing point;

one gets the impression that most of our recent leaders have had a sign behind their desks which reads: 'The buck stops somewhere else.' It is now normal for politicians to duckshove the blame for their own shortcomings back to the public service, which appears to accept its role as an Aunt Sally more or less philosophically; after all, in spite of the constant stream of complaints the shiny bums never get fired, mainly because if they did they just might start telling the truth about what went on.

On top of this it is now considered acceptable – indeed, almost compulsory – for incoming governments to politicise the upper reaches of the public service to such an extent that they have almost become subsidiaries of the governing party. Once again Howard has made this into an art form: not only is the executive level of the service itself crammed with like-minded zealots, but ministers have been encouraged to appoint sympathisers to any advisory bodies under their control. The idea of jobs for the boys and the spoils to the victors has always been a reasonably common perk of Australian politics, but successive Howard governments have taken it to an entirely new level. So follow suit immediately. Miss no opportunity to stack everything in sight with your supporters. You will be surprised and gratified to discover how many positions there are to fill.

You will, of course, have already rewarded your political allies and punished any remaining enemies in forming your ministry. But for those whose total lack of talent and personal failings make even a junior ministry out of the question, there are lesser parliamentary posts. In theory the plum jobs of speaker and deputy speaker, not to mention president of the senate, are nominated by the party rooms and voted on by the parliament; but hey, you have the numbers – if you didn't you wouldn't be prime minister. They are ideal spots for disposing of loyal but utterly incompetent allies, and are regularly used as such by both sides of politics. Then there are the whips jobs, perfectly suited to your thick but determined enforcers. You probably won't be able to satisfy everyone, but you can see that your inner group – your republican guard – stays bought, at least for a little while.

Having secured your back, it is time to be gracious and inclusive. Pay lavish tributes to your predecessor; after all, you have knocked him off once, and it would be great if he stayed around so you could do it again. Unfortunately this is unlikely to happen; in these tough times parties usually give losers the bum's rush in short order. But there is no harm in trying. If you describe him as your most formidable opponent, a man you were lucky to beat once and wouldn't like to face again, you just might persuade his colleagues to give him another run. It was at least partly because Menzies was so gushing about Bert Evatt and Arthur Calwell that Labor wheeled the two patsies up against him three times each.

The other thing you need to say immediately is that you will govern for all Australians, including those who voted against you. This is not really a lie; you will indeed govern for all Australians. Neither you nor they have any say in the matter. It's just that when choices have to be made, you will tend to make them in favour of your supporters, or at least those who you think may be persuaded to become your supporters if sufficiently well bribed. In any case, no one will take you terribly seriously. The 'all Australians' line is just part of the ritual you are expected to go through, like answering 'world peace' when you are asked what you want for Christmas. (The British Prime Minister, John Major, once muffed this reply badly; asked the traditional question he replied that a pair of golf socks would be nice. He lost government shortly afterwards.)

In practice, you will probably not want to do too much real governing at all; the more you try, the more chance there is of failure. You are there because you want the job and the power that goes with it and, in the immortal words of Neville Wran, to keep the other bastards out.

You will, however, have to enunciate some sort of program. As always, keep it vague. Once again John Howard springs to mind: he came to office with no discernible platform at all other than to insist that there would never, ever be a GST; when asked by the media what his plans were, he said he wanted everyone to be relaxed and comfortable. The fact that he went on to head one of the most divisive governments in living memory is neither here nor there; he had stated his intentions in a manner which was acceptable as a television grab and as a headline, and this was all the media really expected.

Howard also continued another great tradition: the 'oh golly, the other mob spent all the money and the cupboard is bare' gambit. Ironically, this was first and most effectively used by Bob Hawke in 1983 when he took over from the government in which Howard himself was treasurer; these days it looks a bit threadbare. But it nonetheless enabled Howard to invent the concept of a non-core promise; the election commitment you are entitled to break if you feel like it (how

much we owe that man!). Thus you can always say with indig-
nation and regret that the tax cuts, the roads program, the
massive new expenditure on the environment, the childcare
centres, the great schools and hospitals plan, the chicken in
every pot – all these long-overdue reforms must now be post-
poned because of the profligacy, the irresponsibility, the
criminal mismanagement of your predecessors. And you can
produce the figures to prove it; after all, your own mates have
now been safely installed in the Department of Finance and
the very least they can do to prove their worth is to juggle a
few sets of statistics for you.

You will also need some kind of legislative agenda; sooner
or later you have to call parliament together, bloody nuisance
and impediment to good government as the institution
undoubtedly is, and the buggers will only make trouble if they
don't have something to keep them busy. Fortunately there is
always a stack of procedural bills which can be relied on to fill
in the time while you decide what, if anything, you really want
to do. You probably have a few pet projects of your own in
mind for the first session or two; if not, it is easy to get together
a package of bills which effectively undo most of what your
opponents did in the preceding term. This is not how you
will describe them to the media; rather they constitute an
unprecedented reform package (note that change is always
reform in political terms) which will streamline the cumber-
some processes of government and improve life for all (of
course) Australians. If the worst comes to the worst, start fid-
dling with the taxation acts. This can provide innumerable hours
of harmless fun for politicians, lawyers and accountants while
making absolutely no difference to the state of the economy.

Ah, the economy. Once again it is necessary to engage in a bit of doublethink. The fact is that your ability to control the bloody thing is almost zero. Even before Hawke and Keating elected to take their hands off the steering wheel by deregulating everything that stood still for long enough for them to take an axe to it, what happened in Australia was far less important than what happened in the world outside. With the onset of globalisation, Australia is almost entirely at the mercy of the big players, both governments and corporations, who know little of the place and care less. The most you, your treasurer and all your advisers can achieve is to try to position Australia to ride the good times and apply palliative care during the bad times, and even at this you can expect no more than a 50 per cent success rate.

Nonetheless, one of the modern political imperatives is to appear to be in complete command; to be a Good Economic Manager. This requires considerable front; Paul Keating used to boast that he played the economy like a violin. In fact he was largely playing with himself, but such was his self-confidence that a lot of people believed him until he announced the recession we had to have. This was too much for even the most credulous and Keating became just another witch doctor. It must be said that Peter Costello at least avoided Keating's hubris; he left the real work to Treasury and did largely what he was told, simply claiming credit or avoiding blame as circumstances dictated. But the economy, rather absurdly given its intractability, is still seen as the main game and when it starts going bad, so generally does the government.

Since it is usually beyond your power to correct the aberrations, it is best to have a distraction or two ready for the tough times. The best of all is a nice little war, the classic example being Margaret Thatcher and the Falklands. John Howard's war against terror or against those fleeing terror or both (one of the advantages of distractions is the amount of confusion they can be made to generate) was also a neat ploy. The sight of the prime minister solemnly farewelling our boys in uniform, even on what is a totally cynical political errand, is a never-failing vote winner; it has worked since the days of Billy Hughes, whose virulent militarism earned him the nickname 'The Little Digger', despite the fact that he never went too near actual conflict himself.

If a real live shooting war is not available, the next best thing is a threat: for more than fifty years conservative governments have lived off the Threat from the North in one form or another, whether as the Red Menace, the Yellow Peril, or more recently the Boat People. All that is needed to sell the idea to the gullible is a map: geography shows that when the sprawling mass of Asia disgorges its surplus, the waste matter will be relentlessly drawn south to Australia by the force of gravity. The mere existence of such a threat means that it is not a time for risks, certainly not the kind of risks associated with a return to government by a discredited opposition; the country must be kept in safe hands. And of course, apart from the fear of invasion, there are ongoing economic dangers that can be parlayed into a Threat more or less at will. If things are going well, don't gamble on change; if they're going badly, it's best not to take chances.

When threats have been used up there are other kinds of distractions that can be employed, some of which have their own attraction; moves towards a republic, or reconciliation with Aboriginal Australia were both treated as distractions by the conservatives in opposition, although as prime minister, John Howard has from time to time purported to take them seriously. You yourself, of course, will never be distracted by such puerile tactics; you will remain loftily above the melee, no matter how much the opposition seeks to disrupt the even flow of good government both inside and outside parliament. In the house, affect a manner of lofty disdain although try not to go quite as far as Keating did when he made blibbling noises at the opposition. (Admittedly, he was understandably sick of John Hewson constantly hissing 'You're a loser, Keating' across the table at him.)

And when you get to dominate the parliament, as I am sure you will, avoid overkill. You don't want the other side to swap an ineffective leader for someone who might be more nearly your equal. Gough Whitlam made this mistake with the hapless Bill Snedden in 1975; he humiliated the man to such an extent that the Libs felt themselves forced to replace him with the much-reviled Malcolm Fraser. Whitlam found he had exchanged King Log for King Stork.

As prime minister you will also have to deal much more directly with the rich and powerful. Avoid both excessive arrogance and excessive servility. There seems to be something in the air of Washington that reduces Australian prime ministers to grovelling imbeciles. You will have to go there sooner or later, but do try to negotiate from an upright position – not that they will take any notice of you anyway.

You will also receive the occasional imperious summons from the likes of Kerry Packer and Rupert Murdoch. At least try to make them come to you rather than rushing to obey their call, but remain flexible. While the power of the media is much overstated – no single campaign ever changed the result of a federal election, although some have had an effect at the margins – there is no need to make enemies. There is certainly no point in going to the extremes of John Curtin, who, when threatened by one of the moguls in 1942, replied bluntly: 'I want you to understand that I obey nobody else but the people of Australia. You may as well know now that you have nothing in the world that I want.' Such heroism is quite unnecessary. Experience shows that very few people really minded when Menzies gave his newspaper mates the rights to run television as well, and no government ever lost an election by allowing a media czar to expand his empire even further. What's more, one may be able to offer you a lucrative position when you leave politics. Bob Hawke actually announced his retirement on *60 Minutes* before becoming, mercifully briefly, a 'reporter' on the same program.

At a lower level it is important to keep the press gallery happy, or at least give them the feeling that they are part of the show – they are never likely to be genuinely satisfied, but they can at least be pacified from time to time. Draw them into your circle; make them believe that they are insiders whose advice is sought and opinions respected. This strategy worked brilliantly for John Curtin during the war years and to a lesser extent for Gough Whitlam during his own ascension; Bob Hawke and Paul Keating both tried it without conspicuous success. The fact that conservative prime ministers have generally been unable to deal with the gallery on its own terms (although once again, John Howard has been a partial exception) has less to do with the journos' own political leanings than with the social ineptness of most Liberals; they are unwilling or unable to mask their contempt for one of the few callings which actually rates below their own in the opinion polls. Once again, a hostile press gallery is seldom in itself fatal, but it is a handicap you can do without.

And if the worst comes to the worst, you can always try to spend your way out of trouble, not just in terms of hand-outs but also in direct advertising. Once again, Howard is the man to thank. In the old days a distinction was made between what was seen as government information and political advertising; the former could be charged to the taxpayer but the latter had to be paid for by the parties involved. The lines were occasionally blurred, but at the very least government information had to be about real things – benefits which were available to the populace because of laws which had actually been passed by parliament. In 1998 Howard changed all that by running a hugely expensive campaign lauding the benefits of the GST ('not a new tax – a new tax system') before bills had even been drafted, let alone introduced into parliament. It was simple electioneering, and Howard, God bless him, got away with it. So now all bets are off: you can raid the public purse with impunity to push any random vote-catcher that crosses the mind of you or your advisers. Howard's even more lavish blitz in 2001 was at least generally about what he laughingly called the achievements of his government; but it still went a fair way to denuding the treasury purely for his own political benefit. Go then, and do likewise.

This is what power is all about; not so much, as George Orwell believed, the power of a boot stamping down on a human face, but the power to pick their pockets, blacken their names, play them for suckers and still somehow retain their votes. Of course, you may do some good in the course of it; a trace of those long-forgotten ideals may come back to you, and you may, in a moment of benevolence, make life momentarily better – at least for some.

But don't get carried away. You didn't sacrifice your youth, your health, probably your marriage and certainly (if the theologians are to be believed) your immortal soul just to be a sentimental old fart. Power was always your aim. You've dreamt it, worked for it, lusted after it and finally achieved it. Now savour it, as does your vicariously satisfied

Uncle Mungo.

SEVENTEEN

In which we delight to exploit the family,
subvert the opposition and wallow in power

My Dear Prime Minister – how good it feels to write that!

You have now, I hope, settled into the Lodge. You can still have your weekends, high days and holidays at Kirribilli House, but don't be too greedy; just a touch of the Uriah Heaps ('umble, very 'umble) always goes down well with the punters, who will balance your other excesses against this rare example of self-denial. You are, of course, still in your political honeymoon, a time when you can get away with almost anything. But be warned: it won't last, and mistakes you make now, while seldom fatal, can still come back to haunt you. Remember, you are in this for the long haul. You are unlikely to beat Bob Menzies' record of 17 relatively untroubled years in the job, but you should at least be looking to rival Bob Hawke's nine.

But speaking of honeymoons reminds me: we have never discussed your family. I assume you have acquired one somewhere along the way; while no longer as essential as they used to be, a wife and a couple of reasonably presentable children are still very useful appendages for a politician, implying as they do that he is heterosexual and responsible. In practice neither may be the case, but as so often applies in politics, perception is more important than reality.

233

There are various ways of going about the tasks (and they should be thought of as tasks: just another part of a politician's progress, like the name change or the air-brushed cv) of matrimony and breeding, all of them with particular advantages and disadvantages. Harold Holt, for instance, took the easy way: he went for the package, taking on Zara and her three stepdaughters as a job lot. This meant he didn't have to do any tiresome child rearing himself, which was just as well; as a serial philanderer his leisure time was already fully occupied. It also gave him an out if any of the children got into trouble: after all he was only the stepfather.

On the other hand, he had failed to prove that he could father children of his own, which is still seen as a bit of a test among the more macho in the community. Thirty years later John Hewson, whose approach to politics seldom rose above the schoolyard, told the public that you could never really trust a man who didn't drive a car or have children, a direct reference to the New South Wales Premier, Bob Carr. Hewson was rightly excoriated for the remark, but he probably struck a nerve or two. Perhaps fortunately, Carr was already considered a bit of an eccentric in the Barry Jones mould, and his failure to contribute to the gene pool was seen as just another conservationist foible.

Hewson himself did less well; having originally married young, he found his first wife something of a handicap in his career and discarded her one Christmas Eve for someone more decorative and ambitious. From a purely pragmatic point of view one can admire his bravado, but the style was a bit too blatant and the timing was terrible. And of course it didn't work; as it turned out neither his new wife nor anyone else could have saved him from the consequences of his political folly. Still, she is probably of value in his present incarnation as a remorseless accumulator of money.

Billy McMahon, whose sexuality was always a matter of prurient speculation, married late, to a socialite who had also been seen as a little out of the ordinary; it was widely regarded as a union of convenience by their friends. This impression was reinforced when, at the start of what was to be an election year in 1972, McMahon announced with great fanfare that Sonia was pregnant with their second child. Jim Killen, who had been sacked from the ministry by McMahon and had not forgiven the prime minister, rang his friend Don Chipp: 'Great news,' Killen enthused. 'Chipp, we are going to screw our way to victory.' Needless to say they didn't, but, rather to everyone's surprise, the marriage survived until McMahon's death.

On the whole the more conventional approach is safer: Whitlam's four children were more or less out of the way by the time he became prime minister, but perhaps unwisely he refused to leave them out of politics altogether. His son Tony stood for and briefly won a federal seat. To Whitlam's enemies, who always numbered quite a few, this was a blatant example of nepotism; but when he appointed his wife Margaret to the board of Commonwealth Hostels all hell broke loose. Whitlam unsuccessfully tried to defuse the issue with a clumsy bit of word play: Margaret, he said, was good in bed and good on the board. This was inevitably interpreted as shameless vulgarity.

John Howard arrived with a younger family, some of whose antics have occasionally caused him a frisson of political concern. But these were more than outweighed by the fact that they gave him and his wife Janette an excuse to appropriate Kirribilli House. And although the Howards' life-long habit of taking family holidays at the retirement village of Hawks Nest – a place so boring that the locals' most stimulating conversation is to reminisce about that wonderful day many years past when a koala walked into the chemist shop – was seen as a trifle unadventurous by some, it always gave rise to splendid stories about the close-knit family, even if the stories were sometimes accompanied by bizarre pictures of Howard walking on the beach in long flannel trousers, socks and open sandals.

Wives also make useful accessories on overseas trips, although some of the more worldly politicians regard their company in the great cities of the world as something like taking a Big Mac to Maxims. There is also a risk that their presence will be seen not as a necessary support for the travelling prime minister, but as a taxpayer-funded indulgence.

So you have a family, which, if nothing else, will be useful for campaign photos and Christmas cards. And you have the top job. But neither of these trophies means that you should let your powers of seduction slide. Far from it. Now is the time to use them most determinedly, and I don't mean simply to bed the hordes of young groupies who will queue up to offer you their nubile young bodies, yum yum. Even though you have by now suborned all those in your own party who are subornable, there remains the problem of the minorities who hold the balance of power in the senate.

This unrepresentative swill, as Paul Keating once described it (and every prime minister from either side of politics would secretly agree with him), almost invariably contains a mish-mash of riffraff, a sprinkling of amateurs, dilettantes, cranks and fanatics who, while knowing they will never have the awesome responsibility of government themselves, seek to subvert the clear mandate of the House of Representatives for their own ends, and my, don't they have fun doing it. Most of the time this doesn't matter; a hostile senate is just another body you can blame for your own failure to deliver your election promises, and while it can frustrate your program, your program is, after all, secondary to your maintaining power, as is everything else.

Most prime ministers thunder that they would rather risk their governments than be lame-duck leaders, but you will notice that remarkably few actually do so. Should they actually call an election on what they nominate as a matter of principle, it is either because they have absolutely no choice in the matter or because their polling has told them they have a very good chance of winning. But in spite of wild hopes and bodgie arithmetic, it is almost impossible for either of the major parties to gain control of the senate, at least in the foreseeable future, so other methods have to be used. This does not necessarily mean the actual physical act perpetrated by Labor's Gareth Evans on the Democrats' Cheryl Kernot, although this should not be ruled out: slipping someone a length, as the Labor federal secretary Gary Gray felicitously put it, may succeed where all else fails. But flattery, wheedling, cajoling, horse-trading, or, in the end, a straight bribe, can achieve much.

Remember, you are the government: *L'état, c'est vous*. You have the keys to the treasury. You can manipulate the staff numbers available to the minors; you can accept or reject their demands for debates about their own neurotic obsessions, you can even help them to set up committees to deal with them. Your opponents, of course, will try to do the same, but you, with your control of public resources, are in an infinitely superior position to deliver real benefits. Use that power.

You will find that the monomaniac Greens and the bleeding heart Democrats, not to mention the knuckle draggers of One Nation and the odd Independent religious maniac will always stuff you around and occasionally, if only to prove to their followers that they have a purpose in life, will feel compelled to put in the boot. But more often than not they will listen to reason, because they know their lives will be pretty bleak if they don't. And there is a new buzzword: if they co-operate, they cease to be mere outsiders, the fairies at the bottom of the garden: they become Relevant. It is a phoney accolade which has won over more than one minority leader: the Democrat Meg Lees and her acquiescence to John Howard's GST springs instantly to mind.

And, should you still fail to get your way, you can always, after sufficient preparation, invoke the ultimate sanction: a double dissolution, which would send every last one of them back to the electorate for a campaign they can ill afford. In fact this is an empty threat, because as the more numerate of those in the minor parties will have worked out (and if they haven't some busybody will tell them), a double dissolution is more likely to improve their position than to diminish it. But the threat applies to your proper opposition as well; to the major party sitting on the other side of the House of Representatives. Assuming the atmosphere is favourable to you (and

obviously you wouldn't be talking about an early election of any kind if it wasn't) they have more to lose than the minors; they face an indefinitely extended period in opposition. And of course if the opposition majority caves in, you don't need the minors at all.

Once again, be ruthless. There are truly terrible powers available to you if you choose to apply them. One of the most fearsome is the setting up of a Royal Commission with terms of reference deliberately designed to discomfit your enemies. This may be quite specific, as was the one Western Australian Premier Richard Court was persuaded to set up in response to allegations involving his predecessor, since transferred to Canberra, Labor's Carmen Lawrence. Rather than take the responsibility himself, John Howard got Court to do his dirty work for him, thereby evading direct blame for what was clearly a political vendetta, a witch-hunt and a kangaroo court. Nonetheless the proceedings, which went on for month after month of public hearings, politically hamstrung federal Labor. Should Lawrence submit to the pressure and stand down from the front bench or should she tough it out? The dilemma divided the party and monopolised the headlines.

Of course, not all diversions are quite as successful. Malcolm Fraser set up a Royal Commission into the notoriously criminal Painters and Dockers Union in the expectation that it would tarnish Labor through the party's association with the union movement as a whole. Unfortunately he forgot the first rule of instigating any form of inquiry, which is that you need to know the results before you put the thing in motion. The commissioner, Frank Costigan, who was in fact something of a Labor sympathiser, quickly confirmed that the union was a bit crook, but then found connections to various tax-avoidance schemes from the big end of town and went after them like a man possessed. A number of Liberal Party heavies were entangled in Costigan's revelations, and in the end John Howard as Fraser's treasurer was forced to bring in retrospective legislation to outlaw some of the more blatant tax scams. It was a political disaster and it was a long time before some of those involved in the corporate shenanigans forgave Howard for his part in it. Indeed, some of the shadier Western Australians still haven't.

One of the many lessons from this fiasco is the need for good advice; if Fraser had been warned about Costigan's leanings in advance much angst would have been avoided. As prime minister you will have a virtually unlimited field of advice available to you, ranging from the whole range of the public service to the resources of the party and its associated organisations – pollsters, advertising agencies and foundations for laundering contributions. You will also be constantly beset by your colleagues who waver between wild elation and the depths of despair depending on the content of the editorial in that morning's edition of their local paper. The trick is to filter out the noise and collect the bits you can use.

In practice you will have a series of cliques around you for different purposes. The first is cabinet itself. In theory cabinet is there to make policy decisions in the best interests of the nation; armed with frank and fearless advice from a proudly independent public service, it concentrates only on the public good and eschews party political considerations, and I am a Dutchman. You have already stacked the public service with your own supporters and your fellow ministers,

while fierce rivals for advancement, are united in the belief
that the national interest is best served by them and them
alone retaining power. Much useful planning comes out of
these meetings, but it needs further distillation.

To this end it is passed up to the Leadership Group,
which consists of you, your deputy, the leader and deputy
from the senate, one or two other senior ministers chosen for
their political cunning rather than their administrative ability,
the party secretary, the party pollster, the party advertising
chief and one or two other apparatchiki of dubious proven-
ance – it is rumoured that there have been times when an
astrologer has been asked to attend, but this seems unlikely. An
economist, perhaps, but this would be the furthest gesture
towards the occult. The Leadership Group is only concerned
with electoral advantage; it doesn't even pretend to give a rat's
arse for the national interest. It is here that the real decisions
will be taken, and the fate of the government (and, as an
unimportant consequence, of the country) determined.

But there is one further step; every prime minister has his
own personal inner circle of trusted friends and colleagues,
usually referred to as the Kitchen Cabinet. It usually includes
a few politicians, a few outsiders (often union officials for
Labor or business executives for the Libs) and even a relative
or two – in John Howard's government his wife Janette was
sometimes referred to as the court of final appeal. From time
to time the personnel changes as one member falls out of
favour or a new confidant is brought in. For the prime minister – you – it is the only group that is really trusted, and he
stands and falls by his choice. Paul Keating's speech writer
Don Watson recounts how, when he first joined the prime

minister's office, he was puzzled by the way certain individuals had unlimited access to the inner sanctum while others, theoretically at least much more senior and important, could never get past the front door. When he was accepted into the charmed circle he learned the reason.

The point about the Kitchen Cabinet is that none of the people involved in it will have the faintest ambition to become prime minister; they are rusted on allies who can therefore be expected to give the best and most objective advice at their command. This doesn't mean that they will always be right; it was Kim Beazley's Kitchen Cabinet that decided on the disastrous small-target strategy that saw him lose two elections and leave the leadership as a failure. It is probably no comfort to him to accept that he was destroyed by incompetence rather than malice. But the survivors of that awful experiment can at least tell each other that they did their best, and constantly do so.

Thus the decision-making process; with all its single-minded pursuit of self-interest and the checks and balances which ensure that no hint of woolly-minded idealism creeps in, is just about the best the system can provide. But in the end you will still have to trust your own instincts. In theory the prime minister can be overruled; in practice this hardly ever happens, and not at all if he is determined on a course of action, however strange it may look to outsiders. And interestingly, with really successful politicians that instinct very often works.

Yet again, there is no better example than John Winston Howard. Howard came to office claiming to be the most conservative leader the Liberal Party had ever had and looked set to prove it. Then, a few months into his prime ministership, a lunatic gunman went on a killing spree at Port Arthur, committing the worst massacre in white Australian history – forget all that black-armband stuff about the Aborigines, in whom there are no votes. Both the left and the right expected the usual reaction from Howard – more law and order, but no interference with the God-given rights of law-abiding citizens to own arsenals up to and including tactical nukes. But to everyone's astonishment the prime minister went for tougher gun control.

It was a masterstroke; it was seen as a difficult and courageous decision, an impression Howard reinforced by appearing at a protest meeting wearing a bulletproof vest. It was seen as confirmation that Howard really would govern for all Australians, that he was not after all a prisoner of the far right. It was seen as the act of a statesman not afraid to take the unpopular course. Did I say unpopular? The polls said that no less than 92 per cent of the populace agreed with him. 92 per cent. You couldn't get that sort of consensus about the Pope being a Catholic. Dissent was limited to a tiny minority of mainly nutters. And yet Howard was able to sell his policy as a brave and uncompromising stroke of leadership rather than the shameless populism it actually was.

That, my boy, is brilliant politics. If you manage anything half as preposterous you are secure on top of the greasy totem poll. And long may you remain there – may the reign of Jack Wentworth Bentley last a thousand years.

Admiring regards from your deeply satisfied uncle,
Mungo.

EPILOGUE

*In which an unexpected development appals
Uncle Mungo until he seizes a solution*

FULL
SUPPORT

LEADERSHIP
CHALLENGE

Jack – No, I can't bring myself to dignify you with that name.

You have reverted. You are Terry Dobbin again. Perhaps you have always really been Terry Dobbin – what is it they say, you can take the boy out of the dobbin but you can't take the dobbin out of the boy … Stop. Calm down. Let us look at this gross act of treachery rationally, you dastard, you poltroon, you wimp and wuss, you, you, you altruist.

So. You have seen the light, have you? You have decided to abandon politics, and you have the gall to blame me for this pusillanimous tergiversation. My letters have shown you how corrupt, venal and downright grubby the whole profession is. Well, let me tell you something, laddie. It wasn't too grubby for Pericles, or Washington, or Churchill, or Lincoln, or Gandhi, or Mandela, to name just a handful. They weren't afraid to get their hands a bit dirty in the pursuit of power, and they have just about become saints as a result.

But you, you want to take the short cut. You're going to pursue a life of prayer and meditation, of peace, love and brown rice. This, you lisp, is the way to inner peace and true power. Pah, I say. Also phooey.

But just a minute, perhaps I am misreading you. Perhaps this new caper has potential after all – not just temporal power, but spiritual as well, and one could lead to the other. I'm sure I've heard something about the Snatchyourhandbag Ashrams, which seem to do all right, and there was this guru in Canada who had a hundred Rolls-Royces or some such ... And the churches aren't exactly broke, and in some places they practically run the joint ... Yes, there could be something in this after all.

It's probably too late to run for Pope, and you won't be able to knock off the Dalai Lama, at least not in this life, but there must be an opening somewhere. And if there isn't, you could always start a new religion – isn't that what that Hubbard fellow did with Scientology? Yes, it's all becoming clearer, my dear chap, I've underestimated you. You have dreams beyond mere national leadership, visions that transcend earthly politics. I see you now as a superhuman figure, a new Messiah. There are no limits. But it will all take careful planning, and once again I can help. For starters, we'll have to do something about your name.

Greetings and obeisance from your most fervent disciple,
Uncle Mungo.

INDEX

MUNGO MacCALLUM